RAIN CATCHER

A Lawyer's Marketing Memoir

JOEL ANKNEY

This book is dedicated to the lawyers who guided me and the clients who engaged me.

Thank you

Contents

Acknowledgments

I do not write alone.

Thank you to Jennifer for everything.

Thanks to Von and Kari for being my sounding board.

Thanks to Janice and Claudia for editorial input.

Thanks to everyone who bought my other books. You gave me the confidence to write this one.

Preface

I celebrated 30 years of private law practice in 2021 and 20 years of solo practice in 2023. Those milestones made me want to give something back to law students and younger lawyers because I am grateful for the help I received from peers and more senior lawyers throughout my career. I had several ideas about how to give back that aligned with my style and personality, and I settled on publishing a book because I enjoy sharing my experiences and ideas through my writing.

Law students and young lawyers often ask me questions about my life as a lawyer, and they seem interested in my responses. They want to understand how I designed my private law practice. My initial idea was to write a book about my entire legal career. I wanted to explain my negative experience with studying law in high school, my process for deciding to attend law school, my process for personal success in law school, my experiences at big law firms, and my experiences as a solo practitioner. I outlined that book and even wrote the first six chapters. But that book seemed too broad. After reading drafts of the initial chapters, I thought: "Who cares about this stuff other than me?" I let the idea for that book simmer for a long time to see if it might blossom into something.

And it did.

While reviewing the outline for my initial idea, I realized many chapters would be about how I have marketed my law practice and obtained clients and new projects inside big law firms and as a solo practitioner. Those chapters seemed to stick out, and I realized they could stand alone and might be more interesting and practical to law students and younger lawyers. So, the idea for *Rain Catcher* was born.

This is a book about marketing tactics, not marketing strategy. I discovered the difference between tactics and strategy while writing this book. According to Allan Dib, the author of *The 1-Page Marketing Plan*, "[s]trategy is the big-picture planning you do prior to the tactics."[1] Developing a marketing strategy involves creating a marketing plan and then developing tactics to achieve the objectives described in the plan.

---

1. Dib, A., 17 (2018) *The 1-Page Marketing Plan: Get New Customers, Make More Money, and Stand Out from the Crowd*. Miami, FL: Successwise.

I've never been very good at creating marketing plans. I have tried from time to time, but creating the plan and implementing it tends to overwhelm me. On the other hand, I don't believe I fall into the trap Allan Dib describes as "string[ing] together a bunch of random tactics in the hope that what [I'm] doing will lead to a [client]."[2]

All my legal marketing tactics have sprung from a desire to get a particular type of legal work. For example, when I volunteered to handle intellectual property work associated with corporate mergers and acquisitions for the big firm I was working at, I quickly gained a desire to want more intellectual property work, so I asked myself what I could do to get more trademark and copyright work.

When I started my solo law practice and wanted to branch into commercial real estate work, I asked myself what I could do to get that type of work. When I wanted to write my first book and was inspired to write about small business acquisitions, I asked myself how to get more of that type of work. My marketing plans have always sprung from a question about how to get more legal work that fulfills me and helps me make money. Then, I develop marketing tactics to pursue the type of work I am targeting. This approach

---

2. *Id.* at 37.

probably annoys marketing professionals as being too simplistic, but it has worked for me for over 30 years.

I have the gift of hindsight when writing. As I wrote *Rain Catcher*, I discovered that, during my career, I have gradually developed successful marketing tactics that align with my personality and capitalize on my strengths as an introvert. Although my marketing tactics have not been grouped by themes during my career, I relate them to you in themed chapters in this book. The approach for sharing my stories does not follow a chronological order, and you will notice as you read that I have worked on multiple marketing tactics simultaneously. My stories about my marketing tactics and results prove that you can craft, adopt, and implement your own successful marketing tactics that will contribute to your success as a lawyer in private practice.

My marketing tactics are not limited by time or technology. Some might try to argue that my tactics were relevant for only the time period in which I used them or with the technology available to me at the time, but my experiences over my three-decade career have proven that these tactics work in any time period with whatever technology is available at the time. Note, however, that differences in time periods and available technology can influence how these tactics are adapted and implemented.

Seasoned lawyers have generously answered my questions and provided guidance throughout my career, especially when I was making significant decisions, such as whether to go to law school, change law firms, relocate, or open a solo practice. Their input helped me, and I want to help you. So, please feel free to contact me if you want to connect and bounce around some questions and ideas about your legal career and marketing.

ONE

The Rain Catcher Mindset

I became proficient at practicing law early in my career, but finding new clients and projects is a never-ending challenge, even after over thirty years of private practice.

I have spent my entire legal career worrying about how to get new clients and business. At big law firms, I worried about having enough work to meet or exceed my billable hour quota to retain my job and get promoted. Since starting my solo practice, I have worried about having a steady supply of fee-paying projects to care for my family and to keep my practice open. This anxiety is ever-present and ever-motivating.

Running a law practice, whether as part of a law firm or as a solo practitioner, is a business, not just a profession. I spend about 50% of a good working day as a solo practitioner doing billable legal work. I spend the rest of the day doing work I can't bill for, such as bookkeeping and accounting, invoicing clients for legal services, responding to emails and voicemails, reading about new developments in the law, and marketing.

I wish I could only practice law because that is the deep work that is most satisfying and financially rewarding to me. The most essential non-legal work I do is marketing. Law school didn't teach me anything about marketing. Promoting and marketing a legal practice (or "rainmaking," as lawyers like to call it) wasn't even mentioned. Law school implied that just being a lawyer would be enough to attract clients. When you think about the business of law, it should be obvious, even to a law student, that a lawyer in private practice needs to be able to get new clients and new projects consistently to survive.

Everything I have learned about legal marketing since I graduated from law school has come from observing the examples of other lawyers, reading marketing books, working with Jennifer (my marketing director), and experimenting with different marketing tactics.

I have heard legal marketing called many things during my career, such as rainmaking, client development, business development, and client acquisition, but to me, legal marketing is simply doing whatever I can to acquire new clients and projects.

Without marketing, my law practice would quickly dry up.

I am a solo practitioner and a transactional lawyer. I don't go to court. My practice consists mainly of small business acquisitions and sales, commercial real estate acquisitions and sales, entity formations, commercial contract drafting and review, and counseling small businesses about various corporate matters. I represent everyday small businesspeople and usually have about 30 active projects on my to-do list at any given time.

The size of my to-do list may sound like I always have a lot of work, but I finish most of these projects quickly. Many projects I handle take less than five hours to complete. For example, it takes me just a few hours to form a limited liability company or to draft or review a contract. Acquisition and sales projects take considerably more time. They might span four to six months, with bursts of activity and lulls during that period.

The work on my desk will probably keep me busy and sustain me financially for about four to six weeks, so the need to refill my to-do list with new clients and projects is always at the top of my mind. I need to fill my to-do list constantly. This need is the never-ending challenge of practicing law, especially as a transactional lawyer in a solo practice.

I have often observed and experienced that the legal profession implies that you must be an extrovert, or at least act like an extrovert, to be a successful marketer of legal services. The implication is that you must be able to schmooze to be a successful lawyer. To me, acting like an extrovert means attending bar and business networking functions, serving on and eventually leading local, state, and even national bar committees, participating in and serving in leadership positions in industry organizations, and entertaining clients and potential clients with activities such as golf, dinners, or even going out for a few beers.

None of those activities align with my personality, so at the beginning of my legal career, I worried that I might not be able to progress because I felt uncomfortable engaging in those types of activities. Through experience and experimentation, however, I learned that I could find clients and legal work by using my strengths as an introvert to discover and adopt marketing tactics that aligned with my personality.

I don't like being in the role of a salesperson. I am not what other lawyers might consider a "rainmaker," and I don't pretend I can teach you to be a rainmaker. The image of a rainmaker seems aggressive to me. It implies that I might have to engage in the types of marketing efforts that I described above.

Instead, I consider myself a "rain catcher." A rain catcher is a barrel positioned at the bottom of a downspout to collect rain to be used instead of water from other sources. A rain catcher operates on the principle that there will be rain and that the rain can be harvested for beneficial uses if the correct collection system is in place.

I have enjoyed a steady flow of legal work during my career, both at big law firms and in my solo practice. My attitude has always been that there is an abundance of legal work for lawyers in private practice, regardless of the size of the law firm where the lawyer works. My strategy has always been to try to have a collection system in place and to position myself where the "rain" falls to catch the legal work and clients around me. I don't have to make it rain; I just need to be around to capture new clients and projects when it "rains."

Seeing myself as a rain catcher instead of a rainmaker takes some pressure off. Being a rain catcher seems more strategic. It means setting up a collection system and remaining aware of opportunities for new legal work as they present themselves. Preparation helps me capitalize on opportunities to market my legal practice when they arise. Being a rain catcher also allows me to focus on my strengths of research and writing, educating, and exercising my curiosity to harvest legal work that will inevitably fall around me.

This book describes how a lawyer in private practice who identifies as an introvert has consistently gotten clients and legal work for over 30 years. It's based on my big law firm and solo practitioner marketing experiences. This book is not a how-to book. I'm not peddling a system or selling secrets. I do not promise you will make a lot of money by using the ideas in this book. No gimmicks here. I cannot teach you to be me. I'm also not advocating that there is only one correct way to market legal services. Instead, this book is a collection of some of my personal experiences that demonstrate how an introverted lawyer has been able to develop and sustain a vibrant private practice without transforming himself into someone inconsistent with his personality.

There is no magic marketing tactic I can teach you that guarantees a big result. To use a baseball analogy, this book is about playing "small ball." My marketing tactics consist of hitting lots of singles and doubles that eventually result in runs rather than trying to swing for the fence each time I create and adopt a marketing tactic.

I will be relating personal experiences and what I've learned from my interactions with other lawyers and businesspeople over the years about how to get more clients and more business. These lessons can apply to lawyers in any size of private law practice. This book is a space where you can pick up tips, get a head start, discover patterns, and possibly adopt tactics that might help you create a "rain collection system" to develop a regular and steady stream of legal work.

Are some of the marketing tactics I use obvious? Of course. But sharing and illustrating my process, my experiences, and their results might give you confidence that these tactics can work for you, too. My experiences might also help you generate your own unique ideas for marketing your law practice.

I relate stories of my personal experiences in this book. Those stories are based on my imperfect memory – 30-plus years in private practice is a long time to remember the details with exactness. My stories are also based on my perception and perspective when they occurred. Someone with me at the same time and place might remember the experience differently because they had a different perception and perspective. Different perspectives and perceptions don't make the experiences I share less true.

I believe that the stories I tell in this book show my colleagues in a good light. I hope they see my inclusion of them in this book as a compliment and an expression of my gratitude for their impact on my legal career. Even so, my perspective on my experiences might not be taken in the positive light I intend. For this reason, I have changed names because I am concerned about how telling a story might be interpreted by those involved. I have also changed client names and identifying information to protect their identities and confidential information. If you can identify an individual or set of circumstances even when I have attempted to describe them without specificity, it will be because that information has already been made public elsewhere.

TWO

Becoming a Lawyer

MY ORIGIN STORY

Y ou should know who I am to understand where I started and how I got to where I am now. My background can give you the confidence needed to explore marketing tactics to help you launch and grow your private law practice.

I have had, and continue to have, a fulfilling legal career. I worked as an associate on the Environmental Law Team at Hunton & Williams and then as an associate and later counsel on the Corporate Law Team at Mays & Valentine (which merged into Troutman Sanders while I worked there). I enjoyed a lot of responsibility at the firms where I worked, supporting and eventually leading environmental regulatory audits at Hunton & Williams and supporting and eventually leading small business acquisitions and intellectual property projects at Mays & Valentine and Troutman Sanders.

I started my solo business and real estate law practice in 2003. In 2017, I published my first book, *Here's the Deal: Everything You Wish a Lawyer Would Tell You About Buying a Small Business*. I'll tell you more about publishing that book in Chapter 13. *Here's the Deal* helped establish me as an authority in the Entrepreneurship through Acquisition community.

This short biographical description paints an incomplete picture, however.

Some of my law school classmates came from families of lawyers. Some were the sons and daughters of well-known regional and national lawyers. Some were named after their lawyer parents, which resulted in instant personal brand recognition. As a result, those classmates had a head start in marketing their law practices. But that isn't my legal lineage, so what you read in this book won't come from that perspective.

I am the first lawyer in my immediate family and the first person in my immediate family to graduate from college.

I grew up in a Maryland suburb of Washington, D.C., as an average kid. My mother and stepfather were civil servants for the U.S. Department of Defense, and my father and stepmother owned and operated a handyman and general contracting business serving customers mainly in the Georgetown area of Washington, D.C. None of my parents graduated from college, although all had some college experience.

I was an average high school student, graduating in the middle of my class with a solid C average. Most of my teenage years were spent hanging out with friends, skateboarding, playing basketball, and listening to and performing music.

Near the end of the summer before the start of my junior year in high school, my mom received a phone call from the school's guidance office. My class schedule had been inadvertently deleted, and my mom and I needed to meet with the guidance counselor to build an entirely new schedule.

Mom and I went to the guidance office late one weekday afternoon. This was a big deal because I'm sure my mom had to leave work early to make the appointment. The guidance office had an entire wall sectioned into a grid from floor to ceiling. Each block in the grid had a class name, teacher name, the number of available seats in the class, and the name of each student signed up for the class. This was before the widespread use of computers, so these names were handwritten on slips of paper and affixed to the wall with magnets. With a glance, we could see which classes were full and which might have space.

I was able to get most of my schedule filled with classes I needed or wanted, but there was one empty block left. The pickings were slim. After a few suggestions (which I can't recall but must have elicited a strong adverse reaction), the guidance counselor pointed out that the Law class had some open seats. I reluctantly agreed to sign up.

My high school Law class was not a significant academic challenge. I had a kind and understanding teacher who seemed interested in giving his students a gentle exposure to the law. But I recall the class was heavily focused on trial work and included some mock trials, which I hated. Frankly, so many years later, I cannot remember why I disliked the class, but I do recall that after taking the class, I swore I would never become a lawyer. And that was the last thought I had about becoming a lawyer until seven years later.

I had no real plan for my future other than attending college because my parents routinely encouraged me to do so. I didn't do anything during my undergraduate education to prepare to go to law school because I never thought about it. I graduated college with a bachelor's degree in organizational psychology with the hopes of starting a career in human resources that would eventually evolve into a role where I would train leadership skills to businesspeople. I also had the idea that, at some point in the future, I would return to college for a Master of Organizational Behavior (MOB).

After college, I couldn't find an entry-level Human Resources job due to an economic downturn. This was distressing. Jennifer and I had married a week before my senior year of college, and we needed jobs after graduation to survive. My college degree didn't seem to be worth much at this point. My father was kind enough to give me a part-time job with his handyman business, which turned into a full-time job when my job search petered out.

I decided to go to law school by degrees. My process was to take one incremental step at a time, with the idea that I could quit or redirect my course at any time.

January 1988 was freezing in the Washington, D.C. area. I recall many days when the temperature was near zero. We worked outside almost daily that month, building fences and small decks and repairing brickwork. While I worked, I couldn't see myself doing this type of work for the rest of my life because I didn't have the necessary mechanical skills or the desire to learn them, which I could see meant that I wasn't committed to the idea. Combining those thoughts with the January weather caused me to consider what might be next for me.

I decided that what might be next would be more education. I had casually spoken of getting an MOB, but before I researched that idea, I had the ignorant, 1980s-influenced thought that an MBA would be a more marketable graduate degree, so I didn't entertain the idea of an MOB anymore. I put that thought out of my mind and cannot remember why I dismissed it so quickly.

I researched MBA programs. I realized that any MBA curriculum would require me to take classes I purposefully avoided during my undergraduate education, such as accounting and financial analysis. Math is one of my weaknesses, and I couldn't stomach voluntarily subjecting myself to that torture. Rather than return to my MOB idea, however, I had the idea to research law schools. Again, I cannot remember what led me to that idea.

As I researched the idea of attending law school, I discovered that the curriculum looked interesting. Constitutional law, criminal law, contracts, and property sounded like classes I would enjoy. This idea hooked me. I signed up for the Law School Admission Test (LSAT), then went to a local bookstore and bought an LSAT prep book. When Jennifer saw the book, she asked me what I was doing and found out about my idea. I wasn't intentionally keeping my idea a secret; it just hadn't come up yet.

I planned to take the LSAT first and then, based on my LSAT results, decide whether to proceed to the next step in the law school application process. I prepped by myself for about nine weeks for the LSAT. It was difficult. The logic problems smelled of math, which worried me because I never felt comfortable with multi-step math problems. I felt my best preparation came from the sample questions and timed practice tests, so I focused more on those.

I woke up early on a cold, crisp mid-winter Saturday morning and drove about an hour to the university where the LSAT was being given. Being back on a college campus felt odd; I felt out of place. I stood in line outside the building where the test was being provided with hundreds of others. Most seemed to be undergraduate students. I felt older, which triggered negative thoughts of falling behind my peers. Most people didn't seem as nervous as me. Many seemed better prepared. I could overhear conversations indicating that many in line had wanted to be lawyers all their lives and saw the LSAT as just another step in their plan. This environment added to my anxiety about pursuing the idea of attending law school.

I remember the test being very challenging. I remember diagramming logic problems on scrap paper with what seemed like insufficient information to figure out the order and colors of the shirts and pants of individuals in a line. Although the test lasted for three hours, the time passed quickly because I was laser-focused. I had no sense about how well or poorly I might have done. Happy to be finished, I drove home in my Honda CRX, blasting a Van Halen cassette tape.

The LSAT results came in the mail weeks later. I decided I had done well enough to proceed to the next step—to apply to law schools and see if I might be accepted.

I discovered that George Washington University would be hosting a law school fair on its campus. GWU was minutes from where I worked with my father in Georgetown. On the day of the fair, I brought a suit to work with me, changed into it at a customer's house, and had my father drop me off at GWU during my lunch hour.

The law school fair was like a job fair. About 100 law schools had set up tables and booths in a GWU ballroom. Each law school had glossy brochures, course catalogs, and paper applications. Representatives from each school staffed the booths to answer questions and encourage students to apply.

At that time, I didn't know anything about law school reputations or rankings. I assumed certain schools, like Harvard and Yale, had highly ranked law schools based on their overall reputations. I browsed the fair without any plan or idea of what schools I might be interested in (or might be able to get into). My only criterion was knowing I wanted to stay on the East Coast, preferably in the mid-Atlantic region.

I decided to pick up information and applications from the University of Maryland-Baltimore, Wake Forest, University of Virginia, and Georgetown Law Schools. I thought the University of Maryland would be my "safe" school – one I had the best chance of getting into. I picked Wake Forest because I was a big ACC basketball fan and liked their team. University of

Virginia and Georgetown were my dream schools because my undergraduate GPA and LSAT score were at the bottom range of their acceptance criteria.

As I was walking toward the exit of the GWU ballroom to meet my father, a woman, who I later learned was the Dean of Admissions, approached me and asked whether I had considered William & Mary Law School. She gently guided me to the William & Mary booth, told me a bit about the school, and gave me the school's brochure and application. I politely stuffed that information into my briefcase (yes, I was dressed in a suit and carrying a briefcase), left the building, changed into my work clothes, and returned to work with my father.

Over the following weeks, I filled out law school applications, wrote essays, got references to write recommendation letters, cut checks for application fees, and mailed off application packets to Maryland, UVA, Georgetown, Wake Forest, and William & Mary. Weeks later, letters came back. I had been accepted to Maryland, Wake Forest, and William & Mary, rejected by Georgetown, and wait-listed by UVA (but so far down the list, it seemed like a gesture to ease the blow of not being accepted).

Law school now seemed a certainty. I tried to learn more. A friend from church, who was a lawyer, answered questions and even took me to court to watch some minor trials. I read Scott Turow's, *One L*. I learned that I didn't have to be a trial lawyer; I could become a transactional lawyer. That was encouraging because I had no desire to go to court. So, I set my sights on becoming a transactional lawyer, even though I didn't know what that meant other than I wouldn't have to go to court.

My extended family had mixed reactions to my decision to attend law school and become a lawyer (I still had no idea what becoming a lawyer meant). My parents were supportive and encouraging. One of my uncles couldn't understand why I would want to be a lawyer and expressed how bad of an idea he thought that was. My grandmother was disappointed that I was leaving my father and his business. None of these reactions made any difference to me. I didn't see what else I could do to secure my future because of the difficulty I had trying to start a career after obtaining my bachelor's degree.

Wake Forest Law School was my first choice. I didn't have a second or third choice. Wake Forest and William & Mary invited Jennifer and me to campus for prospective student weekends. William & Mary's weekend was scheduled earlier than Wake Forest's, so we went there first. The weekend in Williamsburg, Virginia, was overcast, chilly, and dreary. The presentations at the law school were engaging, but I thought my mind was set on Wake Forest.

At the end of the weekend, William & Mary's Dean of Admissions (the same woman who snagged me at the GWU conference) pulled Jennifer and me to the side. She explained that William & Mary was a public school. She also explained that since Jennifer and I had lived in northern Virginia for more than 12 months, I qualified for in-state tuition, which would be about one-fifth of the tuition at Wake Forest (a private school). Well, we had no savings for tuition, so that sealed the deal.

We never visited Wake Forest.

Jennifer and I moved to Williamsburg in August 1988 so I could start law school at William & Mary. In about nine months, I had gone from not considering law school to taking the LSAT, applying to law schools, getting accepted at a few law schools, and starting law school. Many times, I look back and marvel at that whirlwind and all those who helped me through it and the serendipity of William & Mary pulling me into their booth at GWU, scheduling a prospective student weekend earlier than Wake Forest, and caring enough to research and inform me of my qualification for in-state tuition.

I've never felt that being a lawyer is my calling, but I've discovered that I'm pretty good at it, and it provides a comfortable living. I went to law school because I was worried about how I would care for my family when I couldn't find a job after graduating college. The classes also sounded interesting, so I hoped that would keep me engaged. Being a lawyer was a job I thought I could do. Finally, I thought law school might provide me with the skills to care for small business owners like my father.

I am one of those people who thrived during law school. I did well enough to clerk with big law firms during my first and second summers of law school and then receive offers to become an associate at those firms. I spent the first twelve years of my legal career working as an associate and then as counsel in big law firms. Twenty years before writing this book, I started my solo practice.

Practicing law has provided me with a fulfilling career and my family with a comfortable lifestyle. We have had moments when we worried about finances and how we would support ourselves in retirement, but I have no complaints because practicing law has given us a more comfortable life than we probably would have experienced in another career. We have survived and thrived.

I have felt challenged throughout my legal career to align my personality with others' perceptions and expectations of what a lawyer should be and how a lawyer should act. I am an introvert. I don't need a personality test to tell me this, but the ones I have taken confirm it. I have always gained and renewed my energy with quiet time alone, whether reading, writing, walking in nature, or listening to or playing music. Solitude is my sanctuary.

So, why did I decide to become a lawyer?

I had an experience in high school that, in hindsight, helped me decide that becoming a lawyer might allow me to pursue a career where my strengths would be valued. As a senior, my grade for the final semester of my English class hinged on a semester-long research and writing project. For months, I spent many evenings in the Montogomery County Community College library researching and writing a paper about religious symbolism in selected George Bernard Shaw plays. I learned then that research and writing energized me.

Law school and the first few years as a young associate at a big law firm provided me with similar opportunities to spend lots of time alone focused on researching and writing about intriguing legal issues. This arrangement could not last forever, however. I was always aware that I would need to be able to find my own legal work and clients to sustain my legal career if I were to remain in private practice.

My introversion doesn't mean I cannot navigate social and professional situations. I am an introvert with social skills. However, I am much more comfortable holed up in my office researching and writing than at a networking event or entertaining prospective clients. Certain marketing tactics have made me uncomfortable because they seem to conflict with my personality because I don't like tooting my own horn or being the center of attention. So, I have avoided them.

All this is to say that I am not a marketing expert; I didn't have a head start in marketing my law practice from family ties, I don't have any special training about how to market my law practice, and I certainly am not an outgoing salesperson. Still, I have designed a comfortable living by trying different marketing tactics and learning from others.

If I can market my law practice successfully over many years, I know you can, too. You are not me, but you don't need to be. Each lawyer has their unique personality, background, experiences, and skills that will shape their approach to marketing. This book shares what I have done to market my law practice and presents patterns you might follow to help you identify marketing tactics to try in your law practice.

Business is personal, and your marketing tactics should align with your personality. Then, your marketing story can be as genuine and unique as you.

THREE

Clogged Downspout

THE BILLING MENTAL BLOCK

My perspective of the billable hour impacts my marketing efforts. If I can't bill for a task, it will take a back seat to my legal work because billing is directly linked to revenue and, in a law firm, to advancement.

About 18 years after starting my solo law practice, a friend at a boutique law firm in my city called to see if I might be interested in exploring an opportunity to join her firm. The firm consisted of a group of tax lawyers who realized they were referring a lot of business and real estate projects to lawyers outside their firm. They concluded that recruiting a business and real estate lawyer to join their firm would keep that legal work (and the fees from it) inside their firm. Adding a business and real estate lawyer would also keep their clients from establishing relationships with other lawyers, which they hoped would lead to better client retention.

I was interested in exploring the opportunity and accepted an invitation to have lunch with three of the law firm's partners. We hit it off immediately, and I certainly could see myself enjoying being part of their firm. The conversation turned to details about my solo practice, and the first question they asked me was: "How many hours do you bill each year on average?" I answered that I didn't know because I didn't pay much attention to that metric. Instead, I explained that I paid attention to how much revenue I made and my monthly cash flow because those metrics were more relevant to my survival. They were surprised and did not know how to process my apparent disregard for the billable hour.

Of course, my professional life, like so many other lawyers in private practice, is ruled by the billable hour. Billing hours is how I determine the value of my services. It's how I communicate the value of my services to my clients. It's how I get paid. While the practice of law has evolved over the past 30 years to include alternative fee arrangements, I have observed that most alternative fee arrangements are rooted in the billable hour.

For example, I have read books and articles about how to determine alternative fees using formulae that use a lawyer's billable hour rate and an estimation of the number of billable hours to complete a project as factors in the calculation. Even when I quote flat fees, capped fees, or estimates, I do so based on my past fees for similar projects using billable hours. I can't seem to get away from the billable hour. It's always there, either in the foreground or the background.

My productivity has always been measured by others by the number of billable hours I work. This approach was especially true at the big law firms where I worked, where a billable hour quota was the primary performance metric. Knowing that the firm expected me to bill at least 2,000 hours annually led me to calculate how many hours I should be billing each month, week, and day. Tracking my billable hours at a big law firm constantly reminded me whether I was on track to meet my quota. Bonuses, promotions, and even whether the firm would keep me employed were determined almost solely on my billable hours tally. For the first three years of my legal career, I didn't even take a vacation for fear I would set myself too far back on my annual billable hour quota.

I have many thoughts about the effects of the billable hour on lawyer wellness, productivity, creativity, and honesty, but this book is not the proper vehicle to share them. I have, however, observed in my own life that the psychology around the billable hour can harm my approach to marketing because I have been programmed to think and feel that if I'm not billing, I'm not working. For example, marketing was recorded as non-billable work at the law firms where I worked. You weren't rewarded for non-billable work. The implication was that you only worked on marketing efforts when you didn't have billable work. In my experience, non-billable work, including marketing, takes a backseat to billable work. Writing this book even took a backseat many times to my billable work.

This view of billable and non-billable work has created a tremendous psychological barrier in my mind toward marketing, and I don't believe I'm the only lawyer with this issue. It's as if I'm addicted to the billable hour. I have observed many lawyers who turn to marketing only when their billable work is drying up. Their marketing efforts become randomly cyclical – you might even describe them as spasmodic. Those same lawyers then shelve marketing projects when their to-do list is refilled with billable work. I am guilty of living my professional life this way and suspect many lawyers in private practice fall into or follow a similar pattern due to the conditioning they have received about the value of billable versus non-billable hours.

I haven't discovered the solution to overcoming or destroying this psychological barrier, but knowing it exists has helped me remind myself that I need to keep consistently working on marketing, regardless of how much billable work I have. Being aware of this issue helps keep marketing in front of me rather than in the background. As the marketing director of my law practice, Jennifer helps me stay on track with gentle reminders and regular marketing discussions (which sometimes occur informally, away from the office). Jennifer's direction keeps our marketing efforts moving forward, regardless of the amount of billable work on my desk.

Engaging non-lawyers to help you with marketing your law practice, whether it's your partner, spouse, assistant, paralegal, a marketing director inside your law firm, or an outside marketing consultant, will help you establish consistent marketing practices regardless of the amount of billable work on your desk. When you bring others in to help with your marketing, however, you need to explain how your focus on (or addiction to) billable hours may impact your mindset and approach toward scheduling marketing efforts. Non-lawyers who work with you on marketing need to understand your natural, cyclical approach to marketing so they can help you regulate your marketing efforts in fat and lean times. This knowledge might also help them be less frustrated with you when they observe you slacking on marketing efforts because you are focused on billable matters. Understanding the impact the billable hour has on lawyers can improve the relationship between the lawyer and their marketing team.

Hourly rates fluctuate by geographic location and over time. Even though I explained above that revenue, rather than billable hours, is my preferred metric for measuring the health of my law practice, I will use quantities of billable hours, rather than revenue amounts, to report the results of certain marketing tactics described later in this book so that my examples are not outdated or limited by my geographic location. I have used that approach so that you can better estimate how the marketing tactics I share might impact your law practice regardless of when you read this book or where you are located. If you want to quantify the effect a particular marketing tactic might have on your practice in dollar amounts, you simply need to multiply the billable hours I report by your current hourly rate.

FOUR

Measuring Rainfall

ROI

I graduated from law school during a mini-recession. During my 2L summer, Hunton & Williams, the firm where I was spending half my summer, warned its summer clerks to expect that not everyone would receive an offer of employment due to a drop-off in client demand for legal work. I had focused my summer clerkship experience on becoming a commercial real estate lawyer, but when Hunton & Williams made me an offer at the end of my second summer, they made it clear that they could not hire me as a real estate lawyer because there wasn't enough real estate work.

The offer was to become an associate on the Environmental Law Team. My goal of becoming a transactional lawyer was not off to a good start, but I accepted the offer because I liked the firm and the people I would be working with and didn't want to gamble on starting from scratch at the beginning of my third year of law school to find a transactional lawyer position with an unfamiliar law firm.

During my second summer of clerking at Hunton & Williams, I also heard that a large group of lawyers on the Environmental Law Team had recently completed a 10-year nuclear power plant licensing project. In addition, other lawyers in the group had also recently settled several large lawsuits. As a result, many of the lawyers in the practice group were retooling and looking for new clients and projects. I soon learned that there wasn't much legal work waiting for a new associate.

A few months after I started my first lawyer job as an associate in the Environmental Law team at Hunton & Williams, the partners in the group called for an "all hands" meeting. I had observed that the team was informally organized into factions of lawyers who worked on similar projects (e.g., Superfund, hazardous waste management, clean water, clean air) or for specific clients, and each faction tended to have its own approach to finding new clients and projects. An all-hands meeting evidently was a rare event.

The meeting was called because the partners were concerned about how they would find enough new work for all the lawyers on the team. This was disheartening for me because I had already compromised on my career objectives by taking a position on the environmental team instead of searching for a real estate job. Hearing that there wasn't enough work for everyone on the environmental team heightened my anxiety about my decision to join the firm after law school.

We were assembled in one of the large conference rooms on the firm's top floor, all sitting around a large cherrywood boardroom table in our crisp white shirts and ties. The gray-haired partners leading the discussion asked for ideas on how to find more clients and work. Some senior associates suggested creating newsletters or "fax alerts" (before you could blast out emails, we blasted out fax alerts to every fax number the firm had). These suggestions were duly noted.

During a pause in the discussion, I raised my hand, which drew some curious looks, I assume due to my lack of seniority. I asked whether the team had tried any of the suggested business development ideas before. When they answered, "Yes," I asked, "What were the results?" One of the senior partners indicated that he failed to see the relevancy of my question. I explained that it didn't make sense to me to put energy into business development efforts that had been tried before if they hadn't produced results.

I didn't realize that I had spoken out of turn. I think I may have offended some people in the room with my question and explanation, and the partner leading the meeting quickly shifted the discussion away from me.

I felt discounted. The discussion continued without me or my input, and no new or innovative business development ideas were produced. In the end, I recall that the result of the meeting was a conclusion to continue doing what they had done in the past.

I am not relating this experience because I feel it had a bad outcome. Instead, this experience was my first realization that tracking and understanding whether marketing tactics bring in new business is essential. Since then, I have read about this "return on investment" (ROI) principle in many marketing books.

I regularly ask myself whether my marketing tactics are producing results—i.e., whether they are filling my to-do list with new business. I'm not just looking at whether I'm getting results; I'm also looking at the quality of the results. I've tried some marketing tactics that have produced results, but not the results I wanted. I'll share some examples of unwanted results in Chapter 14.

Part of measuring ROI is determining which metrics to use. Will a good ROI from a marketing tactic be measured as an increase in billable hours, an increased number of new clients, types of clients, types of projects, or legal fees? One metric might not be enough to measure ROI accurately. For example, a marketing tactic might return more billable hours, but those hours might be spent working for difficult, energy-draining clients or on projects that don't align with my values, personality, or interests, diminishing the ROI.

I ask myself questions like:

- What type of clients and projects are my marketing tactics attracting?

- Are the projects from clients I enjoy working with?

- Am I getting paid a fair and reasonable fee for my services? and,

- Do I like the type of work I'm doing?

The answers to these questions help me determine where to focus my marketing tactics to attract the types of projects I value, the types of clients I enjoy working with, the clients who value my expertise, and the fees I need to sustain my family and my practice.

Mapping

My mother and stepfather were cartographers for the U.S. Department of Defense. My stepfather helped map the moon for lunar landings, and my mother helped map other areas of military interest in the world. I grew up around maps, and they have always fascinated me because I like to see where things are in relation to each other.

Maps are not only good for determining how to get somewhere but also for determining how you arrived at that place. I have a practice of regularly "mapping" my marketing tactics and their results. When new clients or projects come in, I review how they got to me. I work backward to create a map that helps me understand the origin of the work and the marketing tactics that were the basis for the "route." Mapping my results is one way that helps me evaluate what marketing tactics are working, which can lead me to focus more time, energy, and resources on those effective tactics. I recount a number of "maps" in this book to help you see patterns of marketing tactics that have worked for me.

I am not the best example of implementing the practice of measuring ROI, and I'll blame that on my billable hour mental block described in Chapter 3. I wish I could tell you that I have a thorough system for tracking marketing tactics and results, but the truth is, I mostly keep track of it in my head. My brain is the repository of all my firm's institutional knowledge, so I can file away business development information and call it out when needed.

One benefit of being a solo practitioner is the ability to develop, evaluate, and try new marketing tactics quickly and without any oversight. Even though my system for analyzing the ROI of marketing tactics is imperfect, it's helpful. I can look at a list of my clients and projects and tell you which marketing tactics brought them to me. Likewise, I can recall marketing tactics I experimented with and whether they succeeded or failed (See Chapter 14). Many of those successes and failures are contained in this book because I can recall them vividly. This information helps me determine where to focus my future marketing efforts.

Timelines

There is also a tricky aspect to making decisions based on trackable ROI. Predicting how long it might take to realize the return is difficult. Sometimes, marketing tactics need a chance to mature into valuable results. Many times, you are planting seeds without being able to predict when you will be able to harvest them. Recently, for example, a colleague from almost 20 years ago saw one of my posts on LinkedIn, reconnected, and has since referred several projects to me that have brought in approximately 60 billable hours of legal work with stimulating clients. I couldn't have predicted that the relationship we established when he was a summer clerk at my law firm would lead to a reconnection two decades later that would result in not only a renewed relationship but also new business.

Keeping track of the results of marketing tactics will help you determine where and where not to focus your efforts. I believe there is a certain amount of intuitiveness to these decisions, but you need some basic objective information to fuel your intuition.

Conversely, you must also develop the skill of letting go of marketing tactics that aren't producing the desired results. Being able to let go means accepting sunk costs. I have observed lawyers who will continue to invest in a marketing tactic that doesn't produce results because they've already invested a lot of time, energy, and resources into that tactic. They don't want to lose that investment. Well, I think once you have spent the time, energy, or resources, they are already gone. They don't exist anymore. So, if a marketing tactic isn't producing the desired results, you've already lost that time, energy, and money – they're sunk costs – so why not cut your losses, abandon that tactic, and invest your time, effort, and money into a different tactic? I understand this can be challenging for some. In my experience, although difficult, the quicker you can evaluate and let go of an unproductive marketing tactic, the sooner you can move on to something else that will renew your enthusiasm for developing more business.

FIVE

Put Down Your Umbrella

ASK AND ACCEPT

I wanted to work at a big law firm because I believed there would be plenty of work for me. I believed that large institutional clients would provide a steady stream of legal projects that would trickle down to fill my days with billable hours. That was not the case.

During the summer after my first year of law school, while clerking at a big law firm, I heard that lawyers can be classified into three roles: finders, minders, and grinders. Finders are the rainmakers adept at finding new clients and projects for the firm. Minders cultivate and maintain relationships with existing clients to keep them with the law firm. Grinders put their heads down and get the work done.

I could easily see myself as a grinder and maybe as a minder, but I could not see myself as a finder. I thought the big law firm would be a comfortable space for me to flourish and be recognized as a grinder with minder tendencies. I thought the work would come to me because the firm would recognize and value my grinder abilities.

That's not what happened.

I learned quickly that if I wanted projects inside a big law firm, I needed to seek out and ask for them. Related to that concept, I also learned that if someone asked me to take on a project, I should probably accept it, even if it did not seem to align with my interests or goals. I have experienced many pivotal moments in my career when asking for or accepting projects has blossomed into a steady stream of new projects and clients and helped me develop expertise in areas of law I had not considered when I was a law student or young lawyer.

Here are some of those experiences.

The Audit Team Ask

A few days after sitting for the Virginia bar exam, I spent the morning of my first day as an associate on the Environmental Law Team at Hunton & Williams in orientation, completing paperwork and being welcomed to the firm. This day was the culmination of four years of hard work to get into law school, to graduate from law school, and to secure a job. I was not worried so much about whether I could do quality work for the firm and its clients because I had demonstrated that ability when I was a summer associate, but I was worried about whether there would be enough work to justify my existence at the firm because of a recent economic downturn.

The firm provided lunch after the orientation, and then I was ushered to my office and received my first assignment. I had clerked at the firm during my 1L summer and half of my 2L summer, so I knew the firm and the lawyers in the practice group. I also knew enough about the Environmental Law Team to know that there might not be enough work to keep a new associate busy enough to meet the billable hour quota.

I could tell something was happening when I arrived at my office in the afternoon on my first day because a group of lawyers were in an active discussion in the hallway near my office. I soon learned that Bruce, a mid-level associate, had just resigned. I also learned that before Bruce had announced his resignation, he had been selected to be part of an environmental audit team for one of the firm's biggest clients. The partner (Patrick) and senior associate (Chris) I was assigned to work for were the other two lawyers on that audit team. The hope was that the audits would create a significant amount of billable work for the Environmental Law Team.

When I felt the moment was right that afternoon, I knocked on Chris's office door to ask about being on the audit team. I told him what I had heard about Bruce's resignation and felt confident I could take his place. I asked Chris to ask Patrick if I could be considered for the team. Chris doubted that a first-year associate would have any chance of being on the audit team but said he would ask Patrick.

A few weeks later, Patrick told me I would be on the audit team for the first audit. He also told me, however, that this was temporary until they could identify a mid-level associate to take my place on the team. I went on the first audit, then the second, then the third. I helped draft the audit reports and resolve legal issues identified by the audits. There was never any more discussion about my status on the audit team. The firm never identified a mid-level associate to take my place. Within two years, I was leading environmental audits for a different client. Had I not asked to be on the audit team, I probably would have missed out on hundreds of billable hours of the legal work I did during my first three years of practice. In addition, I would not have gained the expertise I acquired from working on the audit team.

The Intellectual Property Practice Accept

Four years into my career, I lateralled to Mays & Valentine, a mid-size law firm (about 150 lawyers) a few blocks from Hunton & Williams' office in downtown Richmond, Virginia. I switched my practice to corporate law to get into transactional work as I had originally intended when I went to law school. I was recruited to help work on real estate syndication work, but I learned shortly after I joined the firm that the anticipated project never materialized. I was again in a position where I needed to find billable hours.

Two things happened next. First, one of the corporate team partners, who had a reputation for being difficult to work with and wearing out associates, started assigning me work. I didn't say no. Second, a few months after I was hired, a mid-level associate, William, resigned. One of William's responsibilities was to handle intellectual property (IP) matters associated with corporate acquisitions and sales. At the following Monday morning corporate team meeting, our corporate practice group leader asked if anyone would volunteer to take over that responsibility. There was a pregnant pause, and then I indicated I would take it on, even though I knew nothing about it.

Only one other lawyer in the firm knew anything about IP law – Paul. Paul was a younger litigation team partner with some experience registering trademarks. I pumped Paul for training. I frequently met with him to learn about trademark law, and he was gracious with his time and generous with his knowledge. Another lawyer in the firm, Sharon, had been a partner at a North Carolina law firm before moving to Richmond, and she connected me with Taylor, an IP lawyer at her old firm. Taylor became my lifeline, someone I called frequently with questions about the IP projects I worked on. I also attended several intellectual property continuing legal education (CLE) programs, for which the firm generously paid.

As I taught myself and sought guidance from sources outside Mays & Valentine for IP matters, word spread through the firm that I could handle IP projects, and my workload increased. Accepting the opportunity to handle IP matters for business acquisitions and sales resulted in hundreds of billable hours, introduced me to a new practice area, gave me the opportunity to expand the IP practice within the firm, and provided me with a sought-after skill that I would take into my solo practice.

The Hart-Scott-Rodino Practice Accept

William was also responsible for Hart-Scott-Rodino (HSR) filings for Mays & Valentine. An HSR filing is an extensive application filed with the U.S. Department of Justice, Antitrust Division and the U.S. Federal Trade Commission to obtain approval for large mergers and acquisitions. Drafting and prosecuting an HSR application requires significant research of the applicability of the HSR Act to the transaction, the parties to the transaction, and the structure of the transaction; artful drafting of the HSR application; and the payment of a sizeable non-refundable filing fee

($45,000 at the time I was handling HSR filings for the firm).

When the next significant transaction triggering an HSR filing requirement arose, the corporate team asked me to handle the filing. I accepted it to help fill my plate with more work. I look back on this with anxiety because I was a fifth-year associate, there was no one else in the firm to train or supervise me, the fate of the transaction rested on my work, and the $45,000 filing fee was non-refundable, even if I messed up the filing. I learned how to do HSR filings by reviewing examples of filings for prior transactions, research, and trial and error. Each filing would take months to gather and analyze the necessary business information and draft the application. I handled approximately 10 HSR filings over seven years, obtaining approval for every transaction for which I filed. When Mays & Valentine eventually merged with Troutman Sanders, HSR filings were handled by antitrust lawyers in the firm's Atlanta office who specialized in them. I was happy to lose that work and the anxiety associated with it, although it was good while it lasted. Accepting the responsibility to handle HSR filings for Mays & Valentine provided me with hundreds of billable hours, introduced me to a new practice area, gave me the opportunity to work on large transactions, and increased my perceived value inside the law firm.

The Virginia Beach Relocation Ask, then Accept

I was in my sixth year of practice and still wasn't getting enough work to meet my billable hour quota. I was working in the main office of Mays & Valentine in Richmond, Virginia. The firm had recently opened a satellite office in Virginia Beach (about two hours away) by hiring some lateral partners. One of those partners, Carter, was a corporate lawyer billing approximately 2,300 to 2,400 hours a year. That's a crazy amount of work!

I was asked to occasionally work in the Virginia Beach office to help Carter with his workload. I took day trips to Virginia Beach when Carter needed me. Sometimes, I could bring projects back to Richmond for completion. Les, a litigation partner in the Virginia Beach office, suggested Carter hire a mid-level associate to help with his projects and relieve him of some of his billable hours. The firm ran an ad in the Virginia Lawyer's Weekly, a statewide lawyers' newspaper, for a mid-level corporate associate with intellectual property law experience. I happened to read the ad, which described my experience and skills almost exactly.

The next time I was in Virginia Beach for a one-day assignment, I approached Carter, showed him the ad, gave him a copy of my resume, and asked if he would consider me for the position. Moving to Virginia Beach would be great for my career inside Mays & Valentine because, if I could get just an extra 100 to 150 billable hours from Carter each year, I could meet my billable hour quota and set myself up for consideration to become a partner. I thought my willingness to relocate to help the firm might also be another factor to support my bid for partnership.

A few weeks later, I was told that the Virginia Beach office wasn't interested in me for the position because, even though I had the skills they were looking for, they wanted someone who was already located in Virginia Beach who might have an established network of contacts in the area. I thanked Carter and told him I was relieved because after I had given him my resume, I had accepted a time-intensive volunteer position with my church, and I didn't want to move away from Richmond so quickly. I thought that was the end of the discussion.

A few months later, Carter called to see if I still might be interested in the Virginia Beach position. Carter had interviewed several lawyers in the Virginia Beach area but wasn't satisfied with them for one reason or another. I traveled down to Virginia Beach for an interview and was offered the position. For about three months after that, I worked Monday through Wednesday in Virginia Beach and Thursday through Saturday in Richmond. My family eventually moved to Virginia Beach permanently after the school year ended for my children. Professionally, this was a good move for me for several reasons, but ultimately, it did not result in me getting that bump in billable hours I had hoped for. The amount of billable work I received didn't change because, although Carter was willing to give up some work to me, I also lost work from the Richmond office. The gains and losses balanced out, so there was no appreciable net gain on billable hours.

What I did not realize at the time was that the move to Virginia Beach and the clients I would work with there would prepare me to launch my solo practice. I felt more at home in Virginia Beach than in Richmond, I liked working in a small satellite office, and I met some friends and clients that would follow me when I eventually left Troutman Sanders (the successor in a merger with Mays & Valentine) to start my own law practice. Virginia Beach also provided my family with personal, athletic, and educational opportunities and experiences they would not have gotten elsewhere, so I don't regret the move.

The Solo Guidance Ask

I came home one night from Troutman Sanders in a down mood about four years after moving to Virginia Beach. I had been passed over for partner three times because I couldn't meet the billable hour quota and because I "spent too much time with my family and on other outside activities" (that's an actual quote from the email I received from Carter, the second time I was passed over for partner). I made a lot of money for the firm. My actualization rate (the number of billable hours collected versus recorded) was around 95%, which I understood was at the high end for lawyers at the firm, and I provided some specific skills the firm valued (e.g., intellectual property, Hart-Scott-Rodino, entertainment law, and small business mergers and acquisitions), so I was encouraged to stay by being moved to a salaried counsel position. Even though this promotion may have benefited the firm, I was discouraged, and it wasn't a good fit for my mental well-being.

Jennifer could tell I was not doing well and asked me what next step in my career might benefit me. I told her that deep in my mind, I had always been intrigued by the idea of opening my own law practice. We talked about what it would take financially to do that and started working on building our savings to make that a reality. I started working out what other things I would need to do to launch a solo law practice. I saw an advertisement for a day-long continuing legal education seminar about opening your own law practice. Without any explanation, I took a day of vacation from work and attended the CLE.

One of the presenters at the CLE, Brad, was someone I recognized from my neighborhood. I knew his wife worked with Jennifer in the elementary school's PTA, but I didn't know his name or anything about his practice. The class took a break at the end of Brad's presentation. I followed him out of the room, introduced myself, expressed my desire to open my own practice, and asked if I could take him to lunch to ask about his experiences with launching and running a solo practice. Brad agreed, and we had a series of lunches, during which I asked him and his law partner every question I could think of. Brad was gracious enough to help me, and we eventually shared office space for about seven years. Brad also became one of my most significant referral sources for the first 15 years of my solo practice, resulting in hundreds of billable hours and expanding my network of contacts in Virginia Beach. His gracious support was one of the key factors that helped me launch and maintain a successful solo law practice. I cannot imagine what would have happened if I had not asked Brad to go to lunch.

The Ad Agency Ask

Trademark and copyright matters were some of my favorite projects at Mays & Valentine. When I started my solo practice, one of my objectives was to get more trademark and copyright work. From my experience at Mays & Valentine, I was aware that advertising and marketing agencies regularly create trademarks and copyright-protected content for their clients. Therefore, I thought asking local ad agencies for referrals would be a good source of new IP work. I researched the internet to identify about 15 to 20 local ad agencies. I drafted a template of a letter that asked if I could visit their office to introduce myself and my practice. Then I mailed them out.

One ad agency called me and invited me to their office. The office was a renovated house in the old town section of a neighboring city. The agency had been recently launched by some hip, young professionals. They had some big clients (e.g., Coca-Cola), and they allowed me to pitch how a trademark and copyright lawyer could help their clients protect their brands and content. Over the years since our first meeting, this agency has referred several local businesses to me for trademark registration work. The "ask" letter was worth it because it resulted in approximately 100 billable hours over the first few years of my solo practice and helped me establish a relationship with one of the ad agency's founders.

The CPA Ask

Annette, a young dentist, engaged me to help her buy a dental practice in the Washington, D.C., metropolitan area. She was concerned about whether the purchase price was accurate and asked for my input on the valuation of the dental practice. I asked Annette if she had a CPA. She did. I suggested she share the practice's financial information with her CPA, Maria, and ask for a gut reaction about whether the purchase price reflected the estimated value of the practice. A few days later, we spent some time on the phone with Maria, and she gave a clear and concise explanation about why the purchase price was too high. Annette reluctantly decided not to buy the practice based on Maria's input.

I was impressed with Maria's straightforward and practical approach to providing advice. I contacted her soon after Annette terminated the deal and asked if we could meet. Maria and I had lunch, and I asked whether I could refer clients to her because clients often ask me to suggest a CPA to help with their business or transaction. Of course, she said, "yes." My referral relationship with Maria has lasted over a decade and continues to this day. We have referred many clients to each other, many times working as a team on a business startup, acquisition, or sale. Maria's referrals have resulted in hundreds of billable hours for me. The relationship has been beneficial to both of us and our clients.

I often ask clients who they use for other professional or business services. If my client is happy with their service, I feel more comfortable referring other clients to those contacts. Referring clients to these professionals often creates a reciprocal referral relationship, resulting in new clients and projects. Opportunities to acquire new clients and legal work exist all around you. You increase your chances of capturing those opportunities by heightening your awareness of them and asking for the work when you identify the opportunity.

I am a big believer in telling people about my professional interests and asking for opportunities to pursue them. I've never seen much risk in doing so because the worst thing that can happen is that I will be told, "no." Even when I am told "no," I still attempt to create a positive outcome with a follow-up question, such as, "Thanks for your consideration. This is an area I'm interested in, so if you have another project like this in the future, will you please consider using me for it?"

Each of the ask-or-accept experiences described above was a pivotal moment in my career because they brought me more legal work that maintained my value to the law firms I worked in. These projects helped me come closer to my billable hour quota, provided work I was genuinely interested in, expanded my expertise, and, unbeknownst to me at the time, helped me establish relationships with clients and referral sources who would follow me when I opened my own law practice. They also provided me with experiences that would give me confidence to launch my solo law practice.

Finding the courage to reach outside yourself and ask for legal work can be challenging. The first ask is the most difficult, especially if you get a "no" answer. Rejection can dampen your courage. But if you persist, you will succeed; you will get new clients and legal work.

My courage to ask and accept initially originated mainly from my fear of not having enough work and how a lack of work might affect my employment. It was a survival tactic. After seeing the positive results that asking for and accepting projects brought to me, I did not need as much courage for subsequent "asks" as I needed to get started because I was more confident in the outcomes of my efforts.

Legal work is all around you. You've got nothing to lose by asking for opportunities and accepting those presented to you (assuming you are interested in them - I would never suggest you accept something that turns you off or goes against your personality or core values). So, experiment with asking for and accepting work when presented to you and observe the results. Then, ask for more.

SIX

Focus on the Rain You've Collected

THE WORK ON YOUR DESK

Shortly after the all-hands environmental team meeting described in Chapter 4, I was at lunch with Patrick and Chris, my supervising partner and supervising senior associate, respectively. We had a few minutes to chat, and the topic of the all-hands meeting came up. I can't remember if Patrick was at the all-hands meeting (if he was, I don't believe he made any comments), but Patrick discounted the meeting as a waste of time and shared that, in his opinion, the best marketing you could do was "the work on your desk." In other words, if you want more work, do your existing work well and clients will give you more work and spread the word to others about the quality of your work.

I internalized this advice and have found that it is one of the purest forms of marketing. Doing a good job with the work on my desk has led to a lot of new work for me, both in big firms and as a solo practitioner.

The Consulting Firm

While working as a corporate lawyer at Troutman Sanders, a small project from a new client came to Carter, my supervising partner. Carter assigned the project to me.

A former high-profile executive of a US government agency wanted to restructure the ownership of the consulting firm he founded after exiting government work. I listened to his input, advised him on an approach, and drafted the documents necessary to achieve his objectives. I cannot describe with any specificity what magic I worked on this project, but the client was very pleased and continued to return to me for many years with many more projects related to corporate ownership restructuring, the exit of a retiring executive, software and copyright projects, contract drafting and reviewing, litigation defense, and collections. This client even followed me from a big law firm when I opened my solo practice, and brought many projects that helped me in my early solo days. Doing good work for his consulting company resulted in hundreds of billable hours.

Doing a good job for that client with the work on my desk also resulted in two other projects referred to me by the Vice President of the consulting company. The

Vice President belonged to a church community that was purchasing commercial real estate with a large building for several million dollars. Because the Vice President appreciated the results of the work I had done for the consulting firm and the client experience he had with me during those projects, he was influential in getting his church to engage me to represent it in the financing and purchase of the church's new property. Several years later, he referred another client to me for the purchase of a fitness business. These projects resulted in hundreds of billable hours and enjoyable projects for my law practice.

The Artist

At Troutman Sanders, I worked on a team of three lawyers representing a local artist in bringing a copyright infringement lawsuit against a major motion picture studio. I was on the team for my copyright law experience, which I had acquired because I had accepted the corporate team's request for a volunteer to take responsibility for intellectual property matters involved in corporate transactions.

The artist had created and licensed a series of paintings as the cover art for a series of best-selling religious-themed books. The movie studio had released a film that won an Academy Award for Best Visual Effects. The film dealt with religious themes and depicted the main character's afterlife experiences in a series of paintings. Our client alleged that the images in the film looked like his paintings and that the scenes in the movie followed the same chronological order as the covers of the books.

The artist and I became good friends during the representation and remain so. As a result of our relationship, I became the primary client contact for the project and played a part in developing negotiation and settlement strategies and managing client expectations. Ultimately, we negotiated a settlement to the lawsuit. The artist painted each lawyer on the team a painting to express his gratitude for our work.

Because I did a good job with the work on my desk, the artist continued to bring me additional contract, licensing, copyright infringement, and gallery leasing projects for many years, including after I started my own practice. He also referred a family member to me for representation in connection with a book publishing deal and estate issues. I greatly enjoyed working with the artist and his family on these projects, and they resulted in an enriching friendship and hundreds of billable hours.

The Real Estate Broker

My relationship with the artist was a significant personal connection that also helped me create a vibrant commercial real estate practice. One of the artist's friends and patrons needed help with trademark and copyright issues for a family-owned retail business, so the artist referred him to me. The legal issues were complicated, but I worked to resolve them to the patron's satisfaction.

The patron was also a successful commercial real estate broker. He liked working with me in connection with his family's retail business and appreciated the results I was able to achieve. When he discovered that I handled commercial real estate matters, he began referring his real estate clients to me. Over 15 years, he referred three to four significant commercial real estate transactions per year to me on average, and those deals helped grow my real estate practice and reputation. Those transactions also resulted in hundreds of billable hours. More importantly, though, the broker and I have become good friends.

The Client Choice Letter

The time arrived when I felt like I needed to leave the big law firm. After working for big law firms for over a decade, I decided to start a solo practice. I met with Carter, my supervising partner, to deliver my resignation letter. During that meeting, Carter asked me to give him a list of all the clients I was working with and the projects I was working on. He offered to write a letter to each client to give them the choice of going with me or staying with Troutman Sanders. At the time, I thought this was incredibly cocky; I thought Carter offered to do this to show that no one would be interested in following me, but in hindsight, I believe he was looking out for me. Now I realize that he may have simply been fulfilling an ethical duty.

I provided the list, Carter sent the letters, and approximately 25 clients opted to follow me. I believe those who came with me did so, at least partly because of the quality of my work and the relationships we formed while working together. Even though not all of those clients had immediate needs when I started my solo practice, having so many come with me meant I had billable work to do on the day I opened my doors for business. I couldn't have imagined a better start, and many of those clients continued to bring work to my desk over many years, resulting in hundreds of billable hours for my solo practice.

The Sporting Goods Store and its CPA

One of the clients who came with me from Troutman Sanders when I started my solo practice was a sporting goods store with multiple locations. I had previously handled trademark registrations for them at Troutman Sanders, and, initially, that's the type of work they brought to my desk when I started my solo practice. Shortly after I opened my practice, the store's

CPA suggested they create a deferred compensation plan for some of their executives. Based on the quality of my previous intellectual property work, the store's President called me for help. I had never drafted a deferred compensation plan, but I agreed to do so if the CPA would review it before it was finalized and adopted. I knew where to start my research from my experience at Hunton & Williams and Troutman Sanders. I visited a local law school library and found the resources I needed. I sent the draft documents to the CPA for review. His only input was to handwrite the word "perfect" on it and send it to the store's President. Everyone was pleased with the result.

Two things happened next.

First, the CPA referred a non-profit organization to me for help in obtaining financing for and purchasing a new office building for several million dollars for its headquarters. This was another well-paying project at the beginning of my solo practice that also helped establish my commercial real estate practice. In fact, it was the first commercial real estate transaction I ever worked on.

Second, the CPA asked me to draft a letter of introduction for my new law practice. The CPA's office and my law office were in different buildings in the same office park. He drafted a letter of recommendation on his letterhead to include with my letter of introduction, then had his assistant assemble and deliver copies of both letters to every tenant in the office park. Hundreds of businesses received this introductory letter, and at least one tenant engaged me to represent them in lease negotiations for multiple locations.

Contractor, Who is Also a Real Estate Investor

Near the end of my time at Troutman Sanders, a project trickled down to me because it was so small no one else was interested in taking it on. A construction contractor had come across an opportunity to take over ownership of a competitor by assuming a retail store lease and employing the competitor's employees. Other than the assumption of these obligations, no cash would be paid for the business.

The contractor was interested in taking over the competitor because the competitor had access to a manufacturer that would not supply materials to the contractor's business. Dealing with the manufacturer required a delicate touch because the contractor was concerned that the manufacturer would pull out of the deal if they learned that my client was becoming the owner of the competitor. I worked with the contractor to develop a strategy for structuring the transaction in a way that kept the contractor's acquisition, ownership, and subsequent operation of the competitor's business confidential.

The contractor was very pleased with the results of my work, and when he received the letter from Troutman Sanders offering a choice to stay with Troutman or to follow me as I opened my solo practice, he chose to follow me.

After opening my solo practice, I learned that the contractor was also a commercial real estate investor. In the first two decades of my solo practice, the contractor engaged me to represent him not only in connection with projects related to his contractor business but also in connection with several commercial real estate acquisitions and sales. These projects resulted in hundreds of billable hours for my law practice.

The Podcast Mention and B-School Referrals

Kelley is a graduate of one of the nation's top MBA schools. After over a decade of consulting experience with a top-tier firm, she decided to purchase an online business selling products in the USA and overseas. She read one of my books (see Chapter 13) and engaged me to represent her for the acquisition. We worked together for over six months and successfully negotiated and closed her acquisition.

A few months after Kelley acquired the business, she was interviewed on a popular podcast about acquisition entrepreneurship. The host asked Kelley who was on her acquisition team. She mentioned me by name and complimented my work. Two acquisition entrepreneurs who heard Kelley's compliment on the podcast subsequently engaged me to help with their acquisitions. In addition, Kelley referred five additional friends and business school classmates to me to help with their acquisitions or sales. In just over 24 months, Kelley's acquisition, podcast mention, and referrals resulted in approximately 250 billable hours for my law practice.

These stories are just a few examples of how I believe I received more work because I focused on the quality of the work on my desk. I have probably received many more projects as the result of the quality of my work, even many that I am not aware of. In the aggregate, these projects have resulted in thousands of billable hours for my law practice, which were especially needed as I started my solo practice. By writing this chapter, I don't mean to imply that a lawyer might not be focusing on the quality of the work on their desk. Instead, I simply want to illustrate that doing good work with the work on your desk leads to more clients and projects. It is a solid investment of time and effort that will result in a significant return.

As an introverted lawyer, I don't regard doing quality, deep legal work as a challenge. In fact, I would rather spend time developing legal strategies, grinding out legal research and writing projects, and managing complex transactions than networking or socializing to try to meet new clients or referral sources. The good news is that there is a role for that type of legal marketing because clients come back for more legal work and refer their friends when their lawyer provides quality legal work on a project. The reality, however, is that this type of legal marketing takes time because the tactic starts with one project, then expands to additional projects in accordance with a client's needs, and as the lawyer builds trust with the client by doing good work on each project. So be patient but optimistic that doing a good job with the work on your desk will pay off by bringing you more work in the future.

SEVEN

Go Where It Rains

I have always been fascinated by my clients' businesses – how they got started, how they operate, how they market, and how they generate revenue. Clients are proud of their businesses and love it when I demonstrate my interest in learning more about them so that I can better serve them. My curiosity about my client's businesses has prompted me to arrange on-site visits to their businesses.

Every time I have visited a client's business, I have immediately received more work. In each instance, I did not wait for the client to invite me but figured out a tactful way to invite myself. No client has ever been offended or even surprised by my self-invitation. All have responded enthusiastically to the idea. A critical aspect of my self-invitation: I always emphasize that the visit is free of charge.

Chemical Compound Manufacturer

When I was a mid-level associate with Mays & Valentine, I was asked to work with a custom chemical compound manufacturer on a variety of routine corporate projects. I established a great relationship with the founder, Anthony, by phone and email, and we worked together for many years without ever meeting in person. Anthony's manufacturing facility was about a two-hour drive from my office. One day, I got the idea to invite myself to the facility because I wanted to meet Anthony in person, and I was curious to learn more about the manufacturing process. Anthony was thrilled that I was interested in visiting his business.

Anthony was the founder, President, and ultimate formulator of "recipes" for the company's custom chemical compounds. He spent most of his day with me explaining the business and providing a guided tour of the manufacturing facility. We had a great time as I walked with him through the dusty and gritty manufacturing facility in my suit and tie and learned about the process of formulating and fabricating custom chemical compounds.

At the end of the day, we sat in Anthony's office chatting. He had piles of files and papers on his desk, and I believe those visual cues helped him remember open legal issues and concerns. He started handing me file after file, asking me to handle new legal projects for the business. I left Anthony's office with a briefcase full of new work.

Anthony called me several months after my visit for more help. He was working on a new patent application with patent lawyers at a big law firm in Washington, D.C. He said he was having difficulty explaining some of the manufacturing processes to the patent lawyers. He paid me to act as an "interpreter" to help the patent lawyers get the information they needed for the patent application. I am not a patent lawyer because I don't have a technical or mechanical background and have not sat for the patent bar exam. As a result, I know very little about patent law. I suggested that Anthony could save money by not having me in the middle, but he insisted that it was more valuable to engage me to help. He told me that the patent lawyers had never visited his facility, so they didn't understand the processes. He trusted me to be the middleman because I had visited and seen the facility and could explain the processes.

Consulting Firm

I began representing a large consulting firm located in northern Virginia when I was working at Troutman Sanders, and they followed me when I opened my solo practice. Their office is about 200 miles from mine, so most of our interactions have been by phone and email. But twice, I have traveled to their office, once in connection with a small lawsuit I defended and won for them, and once to visit their new offices and catch up with the executive with whom I worked. Each visit resulted in receiving new projects.

When I visited to defend the lawsuit in a local court, I ensured I had plenty of time before and after the trial to visit my client's offices. We had lunch together after the trial to discuss how I felt the trial went and how I anticipated the judge would rule. Then, we retired to the founder's office to discuss his business and its future. Being present in person allowed the founder to ask me questions about topics at the top of his mind and to provide additional legal projects to me.

When I visited a few years later to tour their new offices after a recent move and catch up with my contact on the executive team, I learned about new concerns they had with expanded lines of services and products. Many of those concerns were legal issues, and it was natural for them to hand those legal projects off to me before I left.

Data Analytics Company

I helped a friend, Bart, start a data analytics consulting and software development company more than two decades before writing this book. Initially, I lived in the same city as Bart, but shortly after he launched his new business, I moved to a satellite office of the law firm I was working for about two hours away. For many years, Bart engaged me for intellectual property, contract acquisition, and miscellaneous corporate projects based on our personal relationship and the quality of my work.

About 15 years after founding the company, Bart began expanding his business by engaging new executives for the company's management team. He also delegated responsibility for contract negotiations and other legal issues to these new executives. The new executives did not know about the personal relationship between Bart and me. Some even had established relationships with other lawyers in the area, which I was unaware of.

I invited myself to visit the company's office to discuss some contracts they had signed without my involvement that concerned me. Bart was out of town the day I visited, but I was able to meet with the new executives to discuss my concerns about and suggested resolutions to the issues with the contracts. During the meeting, I became aware that the new executives did not know of my history with Bart and the company, which gave me a chance to demonstrate my knowledge of the company, many of its prior transactions, and key legal issues I had helped manage and resolve during the company's life.

The meeting ended well. I was able to gently re-establish my relationship with the company and build a stronger relationship with the new executives as their outside general counsel. As a result, the company engaged me to help work out the contract issues that concerned me and continued to bring me a significant number of new contract projects.

On-site visits have been one of my most powerful and effective marketing efforts. Each visit has been more than worth my time and effort. I have observed, however, that on-site visits are best with clients who can provide ongoing legal work. For example, an on-site visit to a client who engages me for a one-time sale of their business (e.g., because they want to retire) probably won't result in more legal work. Therefore, I suggest you be strategic in selecting which clients to visit based on the possibility of their need for ongoing legal help.

One challenge for me, as a self-described introvert lawyer using site visits as a marketing tactic, is getting invited to the business. I have found that challenge to be mostly in my imagination, however, because most business owners welcome the opportunity to teach their lawyer about their business, especially when they understand that the visit will be free and that doing so can help the lawyer better serve their business.

Pick a client you want more business from. Pitch an on-site visit at no charge with the objective of helping you better serve the client. I have no doubt the client will embrace the idea. Then go, enjoy yourself, ask insightful questions, learn more about your client and their business, and observe how the client gives you more legal work. One non-billable day can turn into hundreds of billable hours.

EIGHT

Increasing the Probability of Rain

CREATING CLIENT CONNECTIONS

People like to be able to call "their lawyer" when they need help with a legal issue, so you should look for opportunities to increase the probability that someone will view you as "their lawyer."

How can a lawyer increase the probability of getting new clients and legal work?

Establish an Ongoing Connection

Seven years into my career, Mays & Valentine relocated me at my suggestion from its main office to a satellite office about 100 miles away. One of the firm's reasons for the relocation was to provide a rainmaking partner, Carter, with the support of a mid-level associate. I had been a corporate lawyer for only four years because I spent the first three years of my career at Hunton & Williams as an environmental lawyer, so I fit the bill. Carter had been billing approximately 2,200 to 2,400 hours each year, and the intent was for me to relieve him of some of those hours so he could have some more time away from work and for me to boost my billable hours to qualify for consideration to become a partner at the firm.

Carter was a transactional lawyer and had started his career at a small law firm. He arrived at Mays & Valentine by lateralling into progressively larger law firms as his practice grew over time. He was very well-known, respected, and liked in the city. He was a great networker and had many friends who were influential businesspeople in our city. Carter was definitely an extroverted lawyer who used many extroverted legal marketing tactics, such as participating in charity golf tournaments with clients and referral sources and meeting potential clients and referral sources in other social settings.

Carter never expressly taught me anything about marketing my legal services, but I observed what I believed to be one of his effective marketing tactics: forming as many corporations and limited liability companies as possible and naming himself as their registered agent.

Mays & Valentine kept hard copy corporate minute books for clients. The main office had so many minute books that it had a dedicated minute book room filled with bookshelves of minute books. When I moved into the satellite office, I immediately noticed that Carter had his own minute book room for the companies he had formed. I was surprised by the number of companies Carter had formed and continued to form. I noticed he took on just about any new business opportunity, regardless of the business's resources or potential for growth. In some instances, I was puzzled about why a small business might engage a big law firm to start its entity when there were so many other more affordable lawyers and service providers that could do so. I have no idea if Carter cut these small businesses a deal on legal fees, but I assume he must have to entice them to bring their business to him.

In Virginia, a corporation or limited liability company must appoint a registered agent. I have observed that it is a common practice for lawyers who are forming the entity to appoint themselves as the registered agent with the client's permission. The corporation or LLC benefits by having a lawyer as a registered agent because the lawyer can help keep the entity in compliance with annual meetings or consents, annual reports to the state, and the payment of annual registration fees to the state. In addition, having a lawyer act as the registered agent can keep the identity of individuals associated with an LLC confidential because only the registered agent's name appears in the public records at the Virginia State Corporation Commission. Lawyers typically charge a nominal flat fee each year for their registered agent services.

I came to realize that by forming hundreds of small companies, and, in most instances, being appointed as their registered agent, Carter had established himself as each company's lawyer. Any time the small business or its owners needed legal work, they would call Carter first, because he was "their lawyer." Many of those small businesses didn't need any additional legal work after their formation. Even those that needed additional legal services didn't need representation on a regular basis. Nevertheless, because Carter had so many small businesses in his minute book room, it was inevitable that a steady stream of legal work came to him because a few of those small businesses would need legal help at any given time.

I adopted the same approach when I opened my solo practice. For the past two decades, I have formed hundreds of corporations and LLCs and am the registered agent for most of them. I am "their lawyer." While I charge a reasonable annual flat fee for my registered agent services, the real payoff is the additional work these clients bring to me. At any given time during the year, a few of these small businesses will need help with:

- Drafting or reviewing a lease,

- Drafting or reviewing a contract,

- An employee issue,

- Collecting payment from a customer,

- Setting up a new entity for another business,

- Drafting a will,

- Buying or selling real estate,

- Settling disputes between the owners, and

- Buying a new business or selling their business.

When they need a lawyer to help with those issues, they remember "their lawyer" and call me.

This marketing tactic aims to ethically create a connection between you and as many clients as possible, which can increase the probability that clients will call you in the future when they need additional legal services.

Look at your practice and determine if there is a service you can offer that connects your client to you in the future, making you "their lawyer."

For example, if you draft wills and trusts for clients, your client might want to name you as an executor, trustee, successor executor, or trustee. This is certainly one way to connect yourself to your client for future work (be sure to check your ethics rules about requirements for being named as an executor or trustee for a client). Even if you aren't named as an executor or trustee in those documents, develop a way to increase the possibility that the client and their heirs will return to you when they need help changing the will or trust, probating the will, or administering the trust. This might entail packaging the signed estate documents in a folder prominently branded with your law firm name and contact information and including multiple business cards that can be distributed to family members.

If you are a trademark lawyer, you can maintain a docket of trademark registration maintenance deadlines and notify each client as a deadline approaches. That notification not only will increase the probability that the client will engage you to do the work to meet the deadline, but also remind the client that you are their lawyer. If you are a collections lawyer, you might suggest your business clients name you in their contracts as the lawyer that the customer will be required to pay if your client sues them to collect payment.

If you are a transactional lawyer, you might add yourself as a party to whom notices must be delivered under contracts that you draft or review for your clients so that you will be notified when an issue arises and be able to reach out to your client to offer your help. If money needs to be held in escrow for a transaction, you might suggest that you act as the escrow agent with the permission of all the parties. Establishing a connection with a client eases them from the challenge of finding a lawyer when a new legal issue arises. They know exactly whom to call – their lawyer.

Audits and Punch Lists

When I was an environmental lawyer at Hunton & Williams, we offered an environmental audit service to large clients. A team of lawyers and engineers would visit a client's manufacturing facility for three to five business days. We would meet with management, methodically walk the facility, learn about the inputs, processes, and waste streams, ask investigative questions, observe, and note our findings. When we returned to our offices, the lawyers and engineers would take a few weeks to draft an audit report for the client describing our findings and recommended resolutions.

When we audited a facility, we inevitably discovered multiple legal issues (usually related to regulatory compliance) that needed resolution. The audits alone were good projects that brought hundreds of billable hours of work to the lawyers involved, but the real marketing benefit of the audits was to identify new legal issues. The results identified in the audit reports became punch lists of legal issues that our clients engaged us to resolve. In most instances, the punch lists would provide projects that would keep us busy for months after the audit had been completed.

Can you offer an audit to a category of clients that might generate a punch list of additional legal work for you? For example, if you draft wills and trusts, you might calendar a date in the future to reach out to your client to offer an estate review to ensure that their estate documents match the changed circumstances of their lives and any changes to applicable laws.

If you are an employment lawyer, you might offer to periodically review a business's employee handbook to help them update it based on changed circumstances or changes to applicable law. If you litigate contract disputes, you might offer to periodically review a business's form contracts to suggest revisions based on new case law or your experiences in enforcing contracts. If you are an intellectual property lawyer, you might offer to audit a client's intellectual property portfolio and licenses to recommend practices for increasing protection, developing a systematic system for registering patents, trademarks, and copyrights, developing better legal documents, or policing potential infringements.

You might be fortunate enough to sell your clients on paying you for the audit, whether at your full rate, a reduced rate, or a flat fee. However, a client may be more likely to agree to an audit if you offer to do it without charge. You will have to calculate whether a free audit will be worth the billable work you might receive as a result of the audit's outcomes. This calculation should consider the magnitude of the audit and the likelihood the client will engage you to handle the recommended resolutions. For example, offering a free audit might not be attractive if the audit will require multiple days and requires you to spend your money on travel, lodging, and meals to visit the client's facility.

The point of this chapter is to bring to your awareness that you can increase the probability that someone will need to engage you at any given time for legal work by creating a simple lawyer/client connection between as many people or businesses as possible before they need that work. The more connections you make, the higher the probability that someone will consider you "their lawyer" and return to you when they need help with a legal issue. Get enough people to consider you to be their lawyer, and you will likely enjoy a steady stream of billable hours.

NINE

Connecting with Community

There's an adage that you should never do business with friends or family, but if I had followed that advice, I would have turned away many clients who helped establish and maintain my law practice. Natural and genuine involvement in one or more communities will create relationships with other community members that can lead to more legal business.

Jennifer and I have volunteered for decades to help with various organizations within our church, children's schools, and community. When our children were young, we volunteered in Cub Scouts and Boy Scouts. Our children were also involved in middle school and high school sports and performed in various music programs. Involvement in these communities has brought us into close contact with many people who have become our friends and have looked to me, from time to time, for legal help.

For example, a young family moved into our church congregation. The parents, Will and Diane, were about the same age as Jennifer and me, and our kids were about the same age, too. We introduced ourselves after services and discovered they had purchased a home around the corner from us. They had moved to our area because Will had been promoted to a junior executive position at his company's corporate headquarters. We became fast friends, getting together for meals and getting our kids together to play.

A few years later, Will's company was purchased, and the buyer installed a new management team. Will was moved to the basement of the office building and understood the implications for his future at the company. He decided to resign and start his own business. There were a lot of legal issues involved in this move. For example, he had an employment agreement that contained broadly worded provisions about the ownership of intellectual property and restrictions on post-employment competition. What exactly did these provisions mean? And were they enforceable? Will engaged me to answer those questions.

Will also needed help forming a corporation, which he engaged me to do. Over 25 years of our friendship, Will returned to me frequently to draft, review, and negotiate key contracts with clients and vendors, to protect trademarks and copyrights, to draft employment agreements and a shareholders' agreement for his executive team, to resolve contract disputes, to collect money from clients, and, eventually, for the sale of the business when he was ready to exit.

When we first met, we simply became friends. Will wasn't a potential client to me, but our personal relationship formed the basis for a mutually beneficial business relationship that spanned 25 years. Until Will sold his company, he was one of my best and largest clients for my solo practice.

Will wasn't the only person I met in the community who was first a friend and then a wonderful client. While volunteering at church, I met a new family that had moved to the area because they had just bought into a well-known dental practice. I had represented one of the other dentists in the practice on some personal matters (he was referred to me by the CPA for the sporting goods store mentioned in Chapter 6). The new dentist, Todd, was just a few years younger than me. One of his sons was the same age as one of my sons, and a few years later, they would become good friends.

Todd soon needed legal help with his dental practice. He felt comfortable calling on me for help because of our friendship. Over the years, I have helped Todd with practice-related commercial real estate acquisitions and investment-related multi-family housing acquisitions. Todd also engages me for patient disputes and other legal issues that arise from his dental practice.

I did not become friends with Todd to win his legal business, but our genuine and natural friendship created a relationship that makes him feel comfortable to call on me when he has legal questions or projects.

Many other members of my church congregation, neighborhood, and school communities have engaged me for legal projects over the years because of the genuine relationships we created before they needed a lawyer. I am not the only lawyer in my congregation, but I am the only business lawyer. As a result of these relationships, I am also often in a position to refer my friends to other lawyers for legal services I don't offer.

Jennifer's community relationships also have resulted in legal work for me. For example, in Chapter 5, I describe how Jennifer's PTA connection with Brad's wife gave me a foundation for introducing myself to him and creating a connection with Brad to help me launch my solo practice.

Be genuine. Don't join a community solely for the purpose of getting legal business. That would be disingenuous. At some point, everyone will see through to your self-serving motivations. Instead, you should recognize that a vibrant, balanced life will involve you in certain communities and that the relationships you create in those communities may naturally help people feel comfortable approaching and engaging you for legal services. So, enjoy your communities and be ready for people to call on you when they need you.

You will likely gravitate to communities based on your interests and values. You might also be introduced to communities because of your circumstances. For example, if you have children, you may be connected to a school community or to communities related to their interests, such as sports teams or performing arts groups. In whatever community you find yourself, establish comfortable friendships and relationships and consider offering to help the community with your strengths.

If you like to write, you might volunteer to help with the community's newsletter or social media accounts. If you like to sew, you might volunteer to help to make costumes for an upcoming performance. If you like mountain biking, hiking, camping, canoeing, or kayaking, you might volunteer to help organize, lead, or support these activities for a community you, your partner, or your child belongs to.

Community involvement that aligns with your personality will naturally create personal relationships that may lead to legal work through direct representation of community members or referrals from them.

TEN

Relationships with Other Rain Catchers

Everyone you work with becomes part of your personal work alumni network. These friends can become some of your best referral sources and some of the best lawyers to whom you can refer work outside your niche.

Big Law Associate

For example, when I worked at a big law firm, I became friends with Sarah, a labor and employment lawyer at the firm. Initially, I asked her to help me with some employment law matters related to my corporate projects. Due to our similar approach to practicing law, Sarah later became a sounding board for questions I had about how to approach firm politics.

Sarah left the firm to start a boutique healthcare law firm with her husband and some other lawyers. Their law firm quickly grew to one of the larger law firms serving healthcare clients in the southeast United States.

I hadn't heard from Sarah for about seven years. By then, I had left Troutman Sanders and was about three years into my solo practice. Sarah called one afternoon with an urgent issue. Her firm had two intellectual property lawyers who resigned that day. One of Sarah's hospital system clients was trying to wrap up a significant, enterprise-wide software license agreement, and she needed immediate help. Sarah remembered my internal lunch and learn presentation at Mays & Valentine on copyright law (see Chapter 11) and called to see if I could help with her software licensing project. Of course, I could. I set aside my work for the day, reviewed the software license agreement, and provided my comments to finish the negotiations. Sarah took those comments to the software vendor, and they were accepted. The license agreement was modified and signed the next day.

A few days later, Sarah's husband, Phillip, one of their law firm's founding partners, invited me to lunch with the firm's managing partner. They offered to hire me as their firm's intellectual property lawyer. While this was a tremendous compliment (and surprise), I value the independence I've gained as a solo practitioner and wasn't sure if I was ready to jump back into a law firm environment. I thought about the offer for a few days.

I learned from Sarah and Phillip that their firm had previously engaged a solo practitioner employment benefits lawyer as an independent contractor to provide employment benefits legal services to their clients. That lawyer used their firm's letterhead and a firm-branded email address to interact with the firm's clients. The healthcare law firm also insured that lawyer under its malpractice insurance policy.

After learning about this relationship, my counterproposal was to enter into the same arrangement with Sarah's and Phillip's law firm to provide intellectual property legal services to their clients. There would be no discount on my hourly rate, but the firm would be free to mark up my rate if they wanted to. In addition, the firm would pay me when invoiced; I wouldn't have to wait until the firm received payment from its client before I got paid.

We signed a short letter agreement with these terms. I became "counsel" for intellectual property matters for Sarah's and Phillip's law firm. That relationship continued for over a decade until I decided to stop offering intellectual property services in my solo practice. In the beginning, Sarah and Phillip sent me a steady stream of work that resulted in 20 to 30 billable hours each month. Over the years, the work gradually waned because Sarah and Phillip hired several lawyers to handle intellectual property matters inside their firm. Nevertheless, this long-term business relationship that sprang from my earlier friendship with a colleague resulted in gaining an anchor client that helped sustain my solo practice for many years.

Big Law Partner

I had a similar experience with another former colleague. Troutman Sanders hired a seasoned banking lawyer, Geoffrey, from another law firm before I left to start my solo practice. He sat a few doors down from me in Troutman Sanders' office. When Geoffrey had some business clients who needed help with acquisitions and contracts, he was directed by another partner to assign those projects to me. I took care of Geoffrey's clients, and he was pleased with my work and the feedback he received from his clients. I left Troutman Sanders about two years after Geoffrey joined the firm.

About 17 years later, Geoffrey called me. He explained that Troutman Sanders had a mandatory retirement age, so he had reluctantly complied with firm policy and retired when he reached that age. Geoffrey quickly got bored of retirement, so he took a position as a part-time lawyer at a local, well-known litigation boutique law firm. He was tasked to handle a broad range of corporate law projects for their clients. Some of Geoffrey's projects were far enough outside his experience that he didn't feel comfortable handling them. He called me initially to co-counsel with him on the sale of a business where the proceeds would be used to buy out business partners and settle business debts. After we successfully closed those transactions, Geoffrey kept calling me, sometimes to co-counsel with him and other times to refer projects directly to me. He also told the litigators in his new law firm about me, and they started referring business and real estate transactions to me. In the first two years of this relationship, the projects they referred to me generated approximately 100 to 150 billable hours of work.

Summer Associate

Summer associates can also be an important part of your personal alumni network.

I was actively involved in managing the summer clerks for the corporate team at Mays & Valentine. My responsibilities included organizing activities where the summer clerks could meet and network with firm lawyers outside the office. I would often ask the summer clerks what activities they would enjoy. For example, one time, we went mountain biking as a group. Another time, one of the summer clerks, Oliver, asked if a few of us could play golf at a professional-quality golf course in the city. I arranged a day of golfing for Oliver and a few other firm lawyers, including me. I remember that none of us were very good and that the course was challenging because we played a few days after a Nike Tour event (the rough was extremely thick). It was great fun.

After graduating from law school, Oliver joined Troutman Sanders as an associate in a different office. He later left the firm to start his own boutique law firm in the Washington, D.C. metro area, serving politicians, political campaigns, and non-profits involved in the election process.

Twenty years after our golf outing, I published my second book, *Before You Leap: Your Legal Guide to Starting a Freelancing Business.* As part of the book launch, I posted about my new book on LinkedIn. Oliver and I were connected on LinkedIn but had not been in contact for twenty years. When Oliver saw my LinkedIn post, he contacted me for a complimentary copy of the book. During that phone call, Oliver also explained that his clients needed help with entity formation and trademark registration projects and that the lawyers at his boutique firm were so busy with political projects that they didn't have the time to handle them. He asked if he could refer or outsource those projects to me. Of course, I said, "Yes."

After I said "yes," Oliver referred entity formation, trademark clearance and registration, and business partner dispute projects to me. In two years, those projects generated approximately 60 to 80 billable hours of work for me. More importantly, I have been able to help a friend and re-establish a relationship.

Big Law Network

Recognizing that you have a personal work alumni network also provides you with great lawyers to refer to. I have found a kinship among lawyers who worked at Hunton & Williams. There are three former Hunton & Williams lawyers in my area to whom I try to refer projects outside my area of expertise because I know that Hunton & Williams-trained lawyers provide quality legal services. I didn't even meet two of those lawyers until years after I left Hunton & Williams. We have probably referred 80 to 100 billable hours of projects back and forth with each other since establishing the Hunton & Williams connection.

Your legal career will span decades. During your career, you will work with lots of lawyers, and, from time to time, people will go their separate ways to pursue other opportunities. My experiences have proven to me that genuine friendships among work colleagues will be remembered and can form the basis for referrals in the future.

ELEVEN

Cast Your Bread on the Water

BE A GENEROUS GURU

A prominent New York City entertainment lawyer, Jerry, joined the Virginia Beach office of Mays & Valentine when I was a mid-level associate. Jerry had been a solo lawyer most of his career and had represented well-known musical artists of the 1960s, 1970s, 1980s, 1990s, and early 2000s. He was a seasoned lawyer, closer to the end of his career, and had decided to move to Virginia Beach for personal reasons.

How could a solo lawyer attract such successful, high-profile music industry clients?

Jerry was generous with his time, talent, knowledge, and expertise. Throughout his career, he regularly spoke at entertainment law seminars across the country. He also taught entertainment law as an adjunct professor at several highly ranked law schools. Jerry was always available to consult with anyone, many times without charge, about entertainment law questions. Jerry was an expert and generous with his knowledge.

When Jerry joined Mays & Valentine, he wanted associate support for his practice. Because I had experience with small business formation, intellectual property, and contract drafting and review, I was fortunate to be asked by Jerry to work with him on many projects. It also helped that I was a music fan and had a respectable amount of music trivia knowledge.

I was curious about how Jerry found high-profile music industry clients. Here are two stories I heard him tell while I worked for him:

First, Jerry was on a panel of speakers at an entertainment law seminar at a large university. A law student from Georgia approached Jerry during a break and introduced himself as someone helping some friends in an up-and-coming local band. The law student felt like the band might break big. The student asked Jerry if he could have one of Jerry's business cards and if he might call Jerry if he ever had any questions about the band. Jerry happily agreed. Shortly after that experience, the student, now a law school graduate, was managing the band and called Jerry to ask if Jerry could help the band with its first major label record deal. Of course, Jerry agreed, which started a lifelong professional and personal relationship between Jerry, one of the most popular bands of the late 1980s and 1990s, and their manager.

Second, at another entertainment law seminar, in much the same way as the first experience, a young lawyer from Virginia approached Jerry during a break, asking for a similar connection. That young lawyer represented a band that would soon become one of the most popular bands of the 1990s. Within a short period of time after the seminar that young lawyer had engaged Jerry to help with the band's first major label record deal. The band and its lawyer continued to engage Jerry for other projects for many years.

The point of these stories is not to illustrate the magnitude of the clients that engaged Jerry, because he had no way of knowing whether either band would experience any success when the connections were made. Jerry's generosity in sharing these experiences with me provided me with an example of how sharing time, knowledge, and experience with others, including other lawyers, can indirectly lead to more legal work. I call Jerry the "Generous Guru," and have attempted to follow his example.

I want to point out that Jerry also taught me that one's generosity must be genuine – i.e., the time, knowledge, and experience you share must be motivated by your desire and intent to help, not by a base objective of getting legal work. If you are not genuine, people will easily identify and see right through your self-serving motivation.

Seeking out opportunities to act as a generous guru has helped me connect with people who have brought me a steady stream of work. My approach is to share my experiences and knowledge through writing and then speaking, when invited, by those who have read my books. You might find other ways to be a generous guru.

Lunch and Learns

Marketing can be a challenge for a young lawyer at a big law firm. One of the big law firms I worked at had a wonderful marketing department that could help any lawyer in the firm with research to identify prospective clients, but this implied to me that marketing meant only bringing in new clients. That seemed like an insurmountable challenge to a young lawyer who didn't have any connections or relationships with individuals or businesses in the local community that might need and be able to afford the services of a big law firm.

When I volunteered to take on intellectual property projects for the Corporate Team at Mays & Valentine and then determined to expand my intellectual property practice, I discovered that many lawyers in the firm were not familiar with intellectual property law and unaware that I could provide intellectual property legal services to firm clients.

The firm regularly scheduled "lunch and learns" for its lawyers in one of its large conference rooms. The firm provided lunch, and a firm lawyer taught those in attendance about a hot topic or case in their practice area. When I first started practicing law, I viewed these luncheons only as educational opportunities. When I was looking to expand my intellectual property law practice, I realized that these luncheons were also internal marketing opportunities.

I asked firm leadership if we could schedule a lunch and learn where I could make a presentation about the fundamentals of trademark and copyright law. They were interested in the topic and felt it would benefit the firm, so the lunch was scheduled. My presentation was so well-received that I didn't get to eat, and we had to cut short questions so everyone could return to work.

Sharing my expertise in intellectual property law with a large group of lawyers inside the big law firm was one of the best marketing tactics for me, as a young lawyer, to increase my visibility and express my desire for more work. The lawyers who attended were now aware of my expertise and started looking to me to help their clients with intellectual property law projects. This lunch helped kickstart the expansion of my intellectual property law practice inside the firm.

Becoming *The* Expert

In 2017, my first self-published book, *Here's the Deal: Everything You Wish a Lawyer Would Tell You About Buying a Small Business*, was released on Amazon (more on that in Chapter 13). Later that year, I received an email from Mark, a professor at the University of Illinois Gies Business School.

He explained that he would be teaching a new Entrepreneurship Through Acquisition (ETA) course in the business school and asked if I would be open to the students using my book as part of the curriculum. Mark also asked if I would be willing to guest lecture about a lawyer's perspective on ETA during one class session. Of course, I was stunned and flattered by the request and agreed. Mark continues to invite me back each school year as a guest speaker in his course.

Being connected to the University of Illinois ETA course because of my book raised my profile, helped me connect with other guest lecturers in the class, and boosted the sales of my book on Amazon. These outcomes have raised my visibility in the ETA and small business mergers and acquisitions communities. As a result, podcast hosts express interest in interviewing me about my book and my small business mergers and acquisitions experience. I have been invited to speak about my book as a guest on ten podcasts for people interested in ETA or small business mergers and acquisitions. These guest appearances led to more billable hours because listeners have contacted me directly to represent them in their small business acquisition or sale.

One of my guest appearances was as a speaker in Walker Deibel's Acquisition Lab course. Walker published *Buy Then Build*, a book on acquisition entrepreneurship, about two years after I published my book. *Buy Then Build* addresses the business perspective of small business mergers and acquisitions, while my book addresses the legal perspective.

Walker has also been a guest lecturer in Mark's University of Illinois ETA course. Our books are often purchased together on Amazon because they cover similar topics from different perspectives.

I recall contacting Walker to introduce myself by emailing him about our books selling together on Amazon. Walker invited me to record a podcast interview for the Acquisition Lab, then later invited me to teach a class about letters of intent to the Acquisition Lab. With my permission, Walker recorded my class and continues using it for each student cohort.

I did not charge for my input to the Acquisition Lab. The relationship with Walker has resulted in several referrals from him to represent clients in small business sales and purchases. In addition, some of Walker's students contact me directly for legal representation after they watch the recorded presentation.

Increased book sales also resulted in a larger audience choosing to buy and read my book. For example, by selling thousands of copies of my book, I have reached many more individuals than I would have without my book. And all those individuals have opted to buy my book because the topic is something they are interested in.

Since publishing *Here's the Deal*, I have received five to eight small business merger and acquisition projects each year from individuals who read my book and contacted me to see if I could represent them in their transactions. Each new merger and acquisition transaction generates approximately 50 to 75 billable hours of work for me. Being a generous guru by self-publishing a book has been my most effective marketing tactic, and I'll talk more about how I write and self-publish books to market my practice in Chapter 13.

Columbia Business School, YouTube, and New Clients

When I checked my email at the beginning of a Friday morning in late February 2023, I noticed two emails from someone claiming to be an adjunct professor at the Columbia Business School. He explained that he had read *Here's the Deal* and was inviting me to speak to his MBA class on Entrepreneurship Through Acquisition. This invitation surprised me so much that I called Jennifer into my office to ask for her reaction. We both thought it was a scam.

We did some research, however, and confirmed that it was a legitimate invitation to speak at Columbia Business School. That evening, I had a video call with the adjunct professor to accept the invitation and discuss the professor's vision for the presentation.

Jennifer and I created a presentation on the legal process of acquiring a small business. We traveled by train to New York City in mid-April at our expense. The presentation went well, and we stayed at Columbia for a few more hours with the professor and several students to discuss ETA legal issues. It was a once-in-a-lifetime experience.

A few months after the Columbia Business School presentation, Jennifer and I decided to turn the presentation into a video on my YouTube channel. The video was about 45 minutes long, so Jennifer developed the idea to chop the video up by topic into short 5-minute video segments. She posted the long-form video and the short-form segments to our law firm's YouTube channel.

Unbeknownst to me, Raj was searching the internet for information about ETA lawyers. He contacted me because he found the video of my Columbia Business School presentation on YouTube. Raj said I was one of the only ETA lawyers he could find and that he greatly appreciated my videos. After an initial video call, Raj engaged me to help him acquire a small business serving the real estate industry.

Writing books, creating videos based on my written content, and speaking live or on a podcast are ways that I implement the generous guru approach in a manner that aligns with my personality. Consider how you might be a generous guru in a manner that aligns with your personality.

If you like to speak or teach, then speak or teach. You might consider teaching a continuing legal education class, becoming an adjunct professor, or speaking to community groups. Or maybe start a YouTube channel where you can "speak" to your audience. If you like to write, then consider how and where you can publish your written content. Then, share your time, knowledge, and experience and observe how more people will want to engage you after you gain their trust and demonstrate your expertise.

TWELVE

Cloud Seeding

MICRO-DOSED WRITING

I like to write, so I have looked for opportunities throughout my career to market my legal services with my writing. This chapter shares some of my successes using short form writing as a marketing tactic.

White Papers

As a young lawyer at a big law firm and one of the only intellectual property lawyers at the firm, I noticed that most of my clients asked the same questions about trademark selection, clearance, and registration. I sat down one weekend at home and drafted a Frequently Asked Questions (FAQs) about Trademarks white paper. I tried to write in plain English (some may question if that is possible for a lawyer) to make the answers as straightforward as possible.

I formatted it in two columns, with the questions in the left column and the corresponding answers in the right column. The white paper included my contact information at the bottom with an offer to answer additional questions the reader might have. The white paper was about four pages long, and I created a digital copy to easily email it to anyone interested.

After that, any time someone contacted me with questions about trademarks, rather than spend 30 to 60 non-billable minutes on the phone with them or persuading them to pay me for a consultation, I would offer to email the white paper to them and then be available for a consultation, if they had any questions after reading it. Everyone I sent the white paper to valued its contents. Most times, no one had follow-up questions. Almost every recipient engaged me to help clear and register their trademarks. The white paper was responsible for at least ten billable hours of work on average for each trademark I was engaged to protect.

Blogs

When I started my solo practice, not many lawyers were blogging because blogging was a new form of communication and marketing, and, based on my experience, lawyers are typically slow to adopt new technology. Lawyers may have been hesitant to blog because it was a non-traditional way to communicate with potential clients, they didn't like or see the value in giving away free information, they didn't understand how blogging might create a following of readers who could become clients, or they might have been concerned about potential ethics issues related to blogging. I had none of those concerns because I believed any potential benefit of blogging far outweighed any perceived risk. I taught myself how to create a blog and then started writing. My blog posts were designed to answer questions clients frequently asked about small business mergers and acquisitions and intellectual property. I published some blog posts (about 20 or so) before I told anyone about my blog, so there would be a volume of content when someone visited my website. One of my first blog posts was an updated version of my Trademark FAQs white paper.

I quickly determined that a blog has no value if no one reads it, so I had to figure out how to drive readers to my blog. I emailed my existing clients, colleagues, and referral sources to introduce the blog to them. For a few clients, I also personalized emails by selecting a particular blog post I thought they might be interested in and including the link to that post in my email, along with a short explanation of why I thought they might be interested.

I also developed a practice of collecting email addresses during the work week from people I interacted with for the first time. So, for example, if I were at a bar or industry networking event, I would add anyone who gave me a business card to my email list. I also added new clients and other businesspeople, such as accountants, whom I met (even by email or phone) while working on projects that week. Each Friday, I would email those new contacts with a short introduction to my blog and a link to a recent blog post. I tried to be respectful by sending only one email introducing the blog and asking the recipient to subscribe. If they didn't subscribe, I did not send them any more emails about the blog.

My first blog was well-received. The emails triggered thoughts in people's minds about legal questions and projects they had but hadn't got around to. Seeing my emails and reading the blog posts caused those clients to engage me for help. In the first month after implementing the process of collecting contact information and sharing valuable content through my blog, my monthly revenue increased by about 33%.

I have continued to create and maintain different blogs since then. Some of those blogs have come and gone (e.g., a blog about intellectual property legal issues for creatives) because they weren't providing an acceptable ROI. Over time, as my practice has developed into more niche areas, my blog has evolved to where I maintain it on my law firm's website to teach about small business merger and acquisition legal issues.

My approach to publicizing my blog has changed, too. I gave up the practice of sending out emails every week some time ago, partly because my volume of billable work increased so much that I stopped spending a lot of time on marketing (see Chapter 3 for an explanation of my mental block to non-billable work). As I identified where my best projects come from, I used LinkedIn as my main platform for publishing links to my blog posts because it reduces time. It is the place I have identified where current and potential clients will most likely see my content. I create a post on LinkedIn each time I publish a blog post that contains a short description of the post and a link to the blog post hosted on my firm's website.

Repurposing Content

I have also used my blog posts as the basis of short videos on YouTube. I use the blog post as a guide for my video presentation; I don't read it word-for-word. I try to keep my videos under five minutes. I use the same approach on LinkedIn to share my video content as I use for my blog posts to direct interested viewers to my YouTube channel.

LinkedIn posts that link to my blog and YouTube channel are great reminders to my virtual network that I'm constantly looking for legal work. In the past two years, this marketing approach has resulted in approximately 100 billable hours in legal work from projects that people engaged me for because they saw a particular post. Those LinkedIn posts have also been instrumental in getting me noticed by podcast hosts who have invited me to be a guest to talk about my books and law practice. Micro-dosed writing and related content creation have been a good ROI and valuable use of my limited marketing resources.

I still email links to blog posts out to clients and colleagues, but usually only when they have asked a question and I know a particular blog post will answer it. In addition, I have created a few blog posts that I use to gather information. For example, I have a blog post about what information a client needs to provide to a lawyer to form a limited liability company. That post is essentially a virtual intake interview. When a client engages me to create an LLC, I simply email a link to the blog post and ask them to email their information back to me. This cuts down on communication time, gets me the information I need, and directs my client to my blog (hopefully, they will poke around and read a few other blog posts while they are there).

Micro-dosed writing is excellent for creating content for prospective and existing clients, colleagues, and referral sources. I have found that people love to have a lawyer interpret and report on legal issues. They also love free information (who doesn't?). A balanced approach to creating and publishing information through blog posts hosted on your website, white papers, social media posts on platforms where your clients are, and emails can be an effective way to establish your expertise, credibility, and trust with your audience, which ultimately should lead to more projects and billable hours.

I have a lot of legal knowledge, thoughts, and opinions stored in my head because I have been practicing law for so long. Many times, I have succumbed to the temptation to create blogs, blog posts, white papers, and social media posts on a wide variety of legal topics (e.g., issues related to small business law, intellectual property law, entertainment law, contract negotiation, drafting, and enforcement, and mergers and acquisitions). I've learned that publishing micro-dosed writing on a wide variety of legal topics confuses your target audience. For example, I have one friend and client who thinks that I only do entertainment law, even though I haven't practiced entertainment law for over 15 years. His perception stems from a conversation we had over 15 years ago about an entertainment project I was handling. Since then, I have handled several significant commercial real estate and business startup projects for him, but he still identifies me as an entertainment lawyer.

Consistent, targeted messaging about your area of law practice enables current and potential clients to recognize the value of bringing business to you. You don't want to create a blog or other content that covers every possible legal issue related to numerous areas of law. That's too broad and confusing to the audience from whom you want business.

Instead, focus your content on a narrow topic. This has been very difficult for me because I started my solo practice by handling a wide variety of business, real estate, and intellectual property law issues. As I've struggled over the years with narrowing the focus of my micro-dosed writing, I have tried to cheat to avoid that objective. For example, I've tried to brand myself as the lawyer who handles all issues related to the "business life cycle" (i.e., from startup to sale) and the lawyer who represents entrepreneurs (using that term broadly to encompass startups, acquisition entrepreneurs, and real estate entrepreneurs). Those "brands" make sense in my mind, but not the minds of most referral sources and prospective clients. These types of "branding" have allowed me to permit myself to write about a wide variety of legal topics as long as I can establish a link between the branding tactic and the topic. But that broadness diluted my message and, as a result, confused my target audience.

A reluctance to narrow my marketing message in my written content is truly based on a fear of missing out on legal projects I can handle and have had experience with. This fear was powerful when I started my solo practice because I needed revenue immediately and felt that I could generate that revenue only if I took almost any business, contract, employment, intellectual property, or real estate project that walked in the door (sometimes I even took on small business and contract disputes that required me to litigate!). As I have matured in my practice, I have slowly been converted to the idea that narrowing my marketing message is the better approach because it establishes me as the expert in that particular area, dispels confusion about what I do, keeps clients satisfied, and brings me the work I enjoy that also pays well.

THIRTEEN

Heavy Downpour

WRITE YOUR "EXPERT" BOOK

Many lawyers dream of writing a book. Why not pursue that dream by writing a book that can grow your law practice?

I cannot recall when I decided that I wanted to write a book, but I can recall the circumstances that led me to write and self-publish a book to market my legal services.

My brother-in-law, Murray, and I were sitting at the water's edge of a beautiful North Carolina beach at sunset. Murray is a physical therapist, and we were talking about our practices. We discovered that both of us wanted to publish a book. Murray loves to golf, and his idea for a book was about physical therapy suggestions for older golfers. I thought I would write a book about the legal issues involved in starting a small business.

A few years later, Jennifer and I were driving across the country for a son's wedding. She asked me what I was reading and thinking about because she knows I am constantly mulling over multiple ideas at any given time. I told her I was reading a book about legal marketing written by another Virginia lawyer (*Renegade Legal Marketing: What Today's Solo and Small Firm Lawyers Do to Survive and Thrive in a World of Marketing Vultures, 800-Pound Gorillas and LegalZoom*, by Ben Glass). The main message I was taking from the book was the author's suggestion that a lawyer should publish a book to create a reputation for themselves as an expert in a particular area of the law. That sounded like a good idea, but I was frustrated because the author did not provide much practical guidance on how to publish a book.

The next summer, I had a marketing research idea that wasn't initially related to my desire to write a book. I wanted to research information about my past clients and projects to help me focus my marketing message. I thought that by understanding the past, I could create a better marketing approach for the future.

One of my sons was working for me during the summer. Rather than use his time to support my legal work, I decided to use his time for marketing research. I created a matrix for information I asked him to collect from my client files for projects I had worked on over the previous ten years. The matrix included items such as the type of project (e.g., business acquisition or sale, business startup, real estate acquisition or sale, trademark registration, etc.) and the amount of legal fees generated by each project. I felt that if I could identify the projects that generated the largest legal fees, I might focus my marketing efforts on getting more of those types of projects.

For many years, I had thought that the bulk of my practice was focused on business startups, and that's what my marketing message had been. However, my son's research provided the data to help me realize that I had a vibrant small business merger and acquisition practice. We discovered that many of my projects were business acquisitions and sales, and those projects also happened to generate the most legal fees per project. Coincidentally, I also liked working on those types of projects more than the business startup projects.

This new realization rekindled my thoughts about writing a book. What if I wrote a book about the legal issues and processes involved in buying or selling a small business? I researched Amazon and Google to determine whether there were other books on this topic. There were several books about the *business* issues involved in buying or selling a small business, but almost none about the related *legal* issues. As part of my research, I also looked for books about the legal issues involved in starting a small business. There were so many books on that topic that I could easily see that adding another book would probably get lost in the crowd and not establish me as an expert on that topic.

This is how the idea for my book, *Here's the Deal: Everything a Lawyer Wants You to Know about Buying a Small Business*, was born. Now, all I needed to do was write, self-publish, and promote the book.

Note that from the beginning, my objective was never to sell a lot of copies of the book. This distinction is essential when evaluating the book's success as a marketing tactic. Instead, my objective was to self-publish a book that could be used for marketing purposes to educate businesspeople about what I do. My plan was to give free copies to referral sources, potential clients, and clients, to establish myself as the small business mergers and acquisitions expert.

When people discover that I have self-published multiple books, they always ask me how I did it. In the following paragraphs, I'm going to describe my process. Your process might look different, but mine may serve as a guide to personalize and build from.

Outline

I work best from an outline, so my first step was to outline the book. I decided to break the merger and acquisition process into stages and to have each stage form the basis for a chapter in the book. I took a few months to develop a single-spaced, seven-page outline. I used the outline as a checklist for writing the book, checking off each topic as I wrote. My outline was a living, working document. While writing, I regularly added handwritten notes to the outline when my drafting triggered new ideas.

Creating Time to Write

My next challenge was to find or create time to write. I thought I could write at the end of the workday or during my evenings at home after my children had wound down and gone to bed. I had that intention for about three months but didn't write a single word because there was either something else to do during my intended writing time or I was just too mentally and physically tired at the end of a workday to spend another hour writing, rather than being with my family or decompressing from the day.

I needed more discipline.

I decided to commit to a writing schedule where I would write in my law office for at least one hour before beginning my work for the day. For example, if I arrived at the office at 7:30 a.m., I would write until approximately 8:30 a.m., then turn to my client work for the rest of the day. This schedule created tension in me because I was doing non-billable work before billable work. This was especially difficult because the morning is my most productive time of the day.

I wrote diligently each day for about seven months and completed about 75% of the first draft. However, the writing schedule started to wear on me, and I wasn't sure how I would push through to the finish. I decided to rent a cottage at a North Carolina beach for a writing retreat to finish the first draft. I took my family along.

While we were at the cottage, I woke up earlier than the rest of my family and wrote for three or four hours each day while everyone got going. Then, I would relax by spending the afternoons and evenings on the beach with my family and discussing some of the things I had written with Jennifer. I was able to finish the first draft by Thursday of the retreat week and felt a deep sense of relief and accomplishment.

Editing

The first draft was now ready for polishing into a final draft. Jennifer and I each read and edited the manuscript multiple times. I also hired two people I knew to edit the book, both of whom had recently graduated with degrees in English and both of whom wanted to pursue a career in publishing. I paid each of them to read and edit my manuscript. The editing and revising process took a few months.

Self-publishing

While we were editing the manuscript for *Here's the Deal*, I created an author's account with Amazon's free self-publishing service (formerly known as "Createspace" and now known as "Kindle Direct Publishing" or "KDP"). I learned what information Createspace would need from me to self-publish my book. I got an ISBN number through Createspace for free. I prepped the Createspace account so that all I needed to do was upload the manuscript and covers.

Interior Formatting

When the manuscript was at the point we considered complete, I used an online service and engaged a freelancer to format the interior of the book, to create the table of contents, and to create an e-book version of the manuscript that met Createspace's standards. Two files were delivered to me: a PDF file of the formatted interior of the book and a file of the electronic version of the book. I then uploaded both of those files to Amazon's self-publishing platform.

Cover

I also engaged another freelancer to create the front, spine, and back covers for the book and the e-book with my input. The freelancer created four initial cover ideas, and after several rounds of input from Jennifer and me, delivered a PDF version of the paperback and e-book covers. I then uploaded those files to Amazon's self-publishing platform.

Publishing

Amazon's online self-publishing platform then guided me through the remaining items for setting up my book for paperback and e-book publication, including setting the prices and granting rights to publish in other countries.

I clicked the last button and *Here's the Deal* was published and available on Amazon in paperback and e-book formats. We immediately announced the release of the book on our social media accounts.

Later, I also engaged a freelance book narrator to record and produce an audiobook version of *Here's the Deal*. This was the most expensive version of the book to publish, but I felt it was needed due to the number of inquiries I was receiving for an audiobook version. We created an ACX account (Amazon's platform for publishing audiobooks), uploaded the cover art and audiobook file, and published the audiobook.

Timeline

Writing and self-publishing a book is a long-game approach to marketing. It took approximately 12 to 18 months from idea conception to the publication of the print and e-book versions of *Here's the Deal*. The audiobook came later. It was a serious, long-term commitment to a marketing tactic.

Promotion

I thought that writing and publishing *Here's the Deal* would be the most challenging part of the process, but like getting clients for a new law practice, promoting the book was something I wasn't prepared for. Soon after publishing *Here's the Deal*, I developed some grassroots ideas for promoting it.

First, I drafted a press release using templates and guidance I found online. Then, I used an online service to disseminate the press release about the book's launch to about 350 media outlets. No one responded, and none of the media outlets published the press release. That was a waste of money.

I also mailed several free copies of the book and the press release to referral sources, colleagues, friends, and clients. I thought distributing the book to those people would help establish my reputation as an expert in small business mergers and acquisitions. Many of my referral sources appreciated the book. It reiterated to them what I did and that I was "the expert." Since distributing free copies, referral sources have often introduced me to their clients as the author of *Here's the Deal* and an expert in this area of law. That type of brand recognition is invaluable!

In addition, I researched the name of the business editor for my metropolitan area's business newspaper and mailed her a free copy of the book and press release. A few weeks later, the editor emailed me asking for an interview. She included a list of questions in her email that she intended to ask in the interview.

I responded with an email containing detailed answers to her questions and a PDF file of the book's cover. She never interviewed me, but instead took the information from my emailed responses and wrote and published an article in the business newspaper announcing the publication of my book, complete with a photo of me and an image of the book's cover.

During the year after *Here's the Deal* was published, a few copies were purchased on Amazon (mostly by friends and family), and I gave out about 100 copies of the book to potential and existing clients. The book was well received and seemed to be creating the personal brand recognition I desired. Then a couple of amazing things happened that accelerated the book's benefit to my practice.

The Original Book Champion

Mark, a professor from the University of Illinois Gies School of Business, emailed me to introduce himself and a new course he would be teaching about Entrepreneurship Through Acquisition (ETA). While preparing the curriculum for the new class, he researched Amazon for books about buying small businesses. He purchased my book and read it.

Mark felt my book was one of the better books written from a lawyer's perspective about how to buy a small business. He indicated that he wanted my permission to use *Here's the Deal* in his course. Of course, I said, "yes." We talked later by phone about his course and my book, and he invited me to guest lecture for one class period.

Since then, I have guest lectured virtually in his class for six semesters and anticipate that future invitations will continue. Mark had become the first champion of my book. His adoption of my book in his ETA class opened the door to wide exposure of my book to the ETA ecosystem.

Coat-Tailing

The use of *Here's the Deal* in the University of Illinois ETA course had an unforeseen and welcomed effect. In addition to purchasing my book, Mark also required his students to purchase two other books for the course. One of those books, the *HBR Guide to Buying a Small Business*, is a well-recognized and well-selling book written by two Harvard business law professors.

The other book, *Buy Then Build*, was published shortly after I published my book but quickly became a bestseller due to the quality of the book and the author's efforts to promote it. Because these three books were purchased together on Amazon at the same time by a sizeable group of people, Amazon's algorithm suggests to any prospective purchaser of one book that the other books are frequently bought together.

As a result, sales of my book on Amazon are indirectly boosted by the promotional efforts of the authors of the other books.

Walker Diebel, the author of *Buy Then Build*, is also a business broker. When I noticed that our books were selling together frequently and that we were both guest lecturers in the University of Illinois ETA course, I contacted him to introduce myself. He invited me to be a guest speaker in his ETA incubator.

As our relationship continued to develop, he started referring his students to me for legal representation for their acquisitions. In the first three years of that referral relationship, new clients referred to me by Walker accounted for approximately 250 billable hours.

Self-Referrals by Readers

Another indirect result of the use of my book in the ETA class is that thousands of copies of *Here's the Deal* have been sold on Amazon and Audible. It has become commonplace for a reader of my book to contact me and ask if I will represent them in the purchase or sale of a small business. At the time I am writing this book, I estimate that new clients who engaged me because they bought and read my book and then sought me out for legal representation have accounted for approximately 1,200 billable hours.

While *Here's the Deal* was gaining notoriety and bringing me business on a national scale, it was also having a significant impact on my practice locally. A local founder of a national business contacted me to see if I might be interested in representing him in five business deals. He had recently left the business he had founded and was gearing up to launch a new business by acquiring other businesses and transforming them into franchises. The big law firm that usually represented him had encountered some potential conflicts of interest and had declined to represent him in those transactions.

The founder asked a local franchise lawyer for a recommendation for a transaction lawyer to represent him in these new deals. The franchise lawyer had read the article about my book in the local business newspaper, purchased my book from Amazon, read it, and had a copy on his desk. In response to the founder's request for a referral, the lawyer showed him my book, told the founder that I was local, and suggested the founder contact me.

The founder engaged me, and I represented him in several acquisitions. He also engaged me for some regulatory work that impacted the corporate structure of his new business. In addition, he referred me to represent a group of buyers purchasing a local minor league sports team. Over three years, and because my book was on someone's desk, the founder's legal projects and referrals accounted for approximately 300 hours of billable work for my practice.

Writing and self-publishing *Here's the Deal* has been the most effective marketing tactic I have adopted in my practice.

Before You Leap

I did not follow quite the same process when writing my second book as I did with my first book, but writing and publishing it was easier because of my first writing experience.

A few years after publishing *Here's the Deal*, I wanted to see if my law school would hire me as an adjunct professor. I had been an adjunct professor at the law school for five years earlier in my career and wanted to return. I spoke with the faculty member responsible for recommending adjunct candidates to the faculty recruitment committee, and he suggested that I pitch a few course ideas to him for consideration.

One afternoon, while traveling home from a client meeting, I stopped by the law school to pitch my ideas to the professor. Most were related to my small business mergers and acquisitions practice, but the professor didn't seem interested in them. My last idea seemed far-fetched; I pitched a course on the legal issues related to starting a freelancing business.

I have helped many freelancers, consultants, and independent contractors start and run their businesses. I described a potential course to the professor on the legal issues freelancers routinely encounter and how I help resolve them. The professor was very interested in this idea and asked me to draft a one-paragraph description that he could share with the faculty recruitment committee. He told me that if the committee liked my idea, the school would probably hire me as an adjunct.

I called Jennifer on my way home to tell her about my pitch meeting. As we talked, I realized that my pitch idea could be the basis for a book. Instead of giving my idea away to the law school, I decided during our phone call that I would self-publish a new book on that topic. Again, the objective of this book would be to establish myself as the expert and to provide my potential clients, referral sources, and clients with a reference book on the topic. I would not write the second book primarily for the purpose of selling copies.

Outlining the second book, entitled *Before You Leap: Your Legal Guide to Starting a Freelancing Business*, followed much the same process as I used in outlining *Here's the Deal*, although the outline for *Before You Leap* was not as detailed as the outline for *Here's the Deal*.

Amtrak: Time to Write

The process for writing *Before You Leap* was much different than the process for writing *Here's the Deal*. One of my sons was graduating from the University of Utah, and I decided to take a train from Virginia to Salt Lake City to travel to his graduation. The train journey took three days each way. The train is a great place for isolation because much of the cross-country trip passes through areas with little or no cell phone service, so you cannot receive or make phone calls or receive or send email.

I took my outline and my laptop and wrote *Before You Leap* during the six days I traveled on the train.

Timeline

We then followed the same process for editing, finalizing, and formatting *Before You Leap* and its covers as we used for *Here's the Deal*. We also engaged the same book narrator to record and produce an audiobook version of *Before You Leap*. Paperback, e-book, and audiobook versions of *Before You Leap* were then self-published and released on Amazon and Audible. It took approximately 12 months from idea conception to the publication of *Before You Leap*. Again, another significant, long-term commitment to a marketing tactic.

Promotion

The primary promotional effort for *Before You Leap* was to announce its launch on LinkedIn. We didn't draft or publish a press release and we didn't send out many complimentary copies. We contacted the business editor who published the article about *Here's the Deal*, but she wasn't interested in writing an article about *Before You Leap*.

One of the results of our LinkedIn announcement was the re-establishment of a friendship with a lawyer who was a summer clerk at Troutman Sanders when I worked there. He contacted me through LinkedIn about the book and I sent him a complimentary copy. He soon called and asked whether he could refer business startup and trademark registration projects to me when his firm was over capacity. Of course, I said, "yes." During the first year of this renewed relationship, my colleague's referrals accounted for approximately 60 billable hours.

In my opinion, *Before You Leap* is well-written and very informative, but no one has championed the book yet in the way Mark championed *Here's the Deal*, so it has not had the same impact on my practice as *Here's the Deal* has. While *Before You Leap* has not yet garnered results similar to those we experienced with *Here's the Deal*, its results to date prove a significant return on our investment of time and money by the resulting amount of billable work and associated revenue.

Write *Your* Book

If you take one marketing idea from this book to build your law practice, it should be to self-publish a book on a legal topic that will establish you as the expert on that topic.

You might think that you need many years of legal experience before you can write a book, but that's not true. You are trained as a lawyer to research and write about complicated legal topics, many of which are new to you, in a detailed and persuasive way. You can use those skills to identify, research, and write an informative and practical book that can help prospective clients. You don't need to be an expert to write the book; researching and writing the book will make you the expert.

A self-published book can be used in so many ways to market your law practice. For example, one of my colleagues asked me how much I paid for each book when my author's discount is applied to the retail price of each copy. When I told him how inexpensive each book costs to me, he recommended I give them away like business cards. I adopted his suggestion and quickly discovered that giving someone a copy of my book is much more impactful than giving them a business card. Giving new clients a copy of your book can also be a great client relationship tool that improves your client's trust in you.

Being an author sets you apart from other lawyers, even those who may have more experience and greater name recognition. When you are at a networking or social event, especially where other lawyers are present, you will probably be the only author in the room. That distinction will attract attention to you, and you will find that others (even other lawyers) will want to establish a relationship with you because of your uniqueness.

If you decide to self-publish a book, you will need to create your own process, but my experience may serve as an example. It looks like this:

- Identify your topic (try to pick something unique or to approach a common issue from a unique angle),

- Outline your book,

- Create and stick to a writing schedule,

- Draft and edit your manuscript,

- Engage others to proof and edit your manuscript,

- Engage a freelancer to format the interior and create the table of contents,

- Engage a freelancer to create your front, spine, and back covers,

- Create a KDP author account,

- Upload your final formatted manuscript and covers to KDP,

- Release your book on Amazon, and

- Create and implement promotional tactics.

Promoting Your New Book

In my experience, promoting the book is the most challenging part of self-publishing. The book won't have much marketing value if no one reads it. This book is not intended to teach you the details of how to promote a self-published book; there are plenty of other books out there that can help. See, for example, *How to Market a Book*, by Joanna Penn.

You may feel that self-publishing a book will give away too much information that you might otherwise be able to charge legal fees for. You may believe that if someone buys or receives a free copy of your book, they won't engage you for legal services. My experience has been the opposite. Readers of my books realize how complex the legal issues discussed in my books are and are more willing to engage a lawyer they trust to help them navigate those issues. Even clients who are traditionally do-it-yourselfers have engaged me after reading one of my books because the book helped them realize that they shouldn't handle legal issues without a lawyer.

You may feel like self-publishing a book won't be as valuable if every lawyer who reads this book publishes their own book. So many lawyers have asked me about my self-publishing process and results since I published my first book, but, to my knowledge, none have published their own books after I've described the process. So, I predict that not many readers of this book will self-publish their own book because the cost in time and the discipline necessary to do so are too great for most. This means that if you follow through with this idea, you will still be unique, which will be a great marketing tool for your law practice.

So, do it. Write your book. You won't regret it, and it may be the best marketing tactic you try.

FOURTEEN

All Thunder, No Rain

ABANDONED TACTICS

I have learned how to get new clients and projects mostly through trial and error. Every other chapter in this book contains stories about my successes. This chapter contains stories about marketing tactics I have tried, but then decided to abandon. They are experiments that didn't work for me.

Jennifer and I spend a lot of time reading books and listening to podcasts about business, marketing, and consumer experiences. This openness to learning sparks new ideas for marketing tactics. We talk about these ideas regularly. Sometimes we share thoughts and make decisions about new marketing tactics during our walks. Other times, those discussions happen on long drives. Eventually, we get around to trying out a new tactic and evaluating its effectiveness.

Here are a few tactics we tried to reach my target audience and then abandoned:

Pricing

When I started my solo practice, I adopted the slogan, "Big Firm Service, Small Firm Price," thinking that I could attract some big law firm clients to engage me because I could provide the same sophistication of legal services as a big law firm, but for a much lower hourly rate. I quickly learned that no one cared about either of those promises.

Clients who want big law firm services want them for a reason. For example, one of my best clients, who had engaged me for many projects, decided to engage a big law firm lawyer for a dispute he was having with his business partner because he felt that the big law firm lawyer's reputation would carry more weight in the negotiations than mine, which would lead to a faster and better resolution for him. He wasn't concerned about the price.

I represented another business in the construction industry owned by two partners. One of the partners decided to retire and wanted to be bought out. The buyout wasn't adversarial, but both partners decided to engage separate big law firms because they thought (without asking me) that the matter was too complicated for a solo practitioner. The big firm lawyers on both sides drafted lengthy contracts and needlessly fought over every detail. They billed so much for their services that the business partners finally had enough and negotiated the buyout terms without the lawyers, then dictated those terms to the lawyers, telling them not to spend any more time negotiating. I learned after the deal was closed that one partner paid approximately $80,000 in legal fees while the other paid over $100,000 in legal fees. I told them I could have done the job effectively for a fraction of the cost.

I discovered that many businesses that could have saved money using my services weren't interested in buying based on price. I also found that clients who shopped for and engaged lawyers based on price were usually the most difficult clients to represent because they had unrealistic demands and expectations. I've since learned about other reasons not to market based on price, including the adage that competing on price is a race to the bottom, but my personal experiences with this tactic were enough to cause me to abandon it.

Non-Personal Branding

My father owned and operated a small, but very successful, handyman and general contracting business. The name of his company was "Ankney Maintenance & Services." When I was in college, I suggested he consider adopting a fancy brand name and logo to "take his business to the next level" (I was young and brash). He explained that his simple rule was to tell people who you are and what you do. This was his approach to personal branding for a service business. I understand now what he meant.

For many years, I was under the false perception that I was a lawyer who represented entrepreneurs and startups. A few years after opening my solo practice, I gave one of my cars to my son headed to college and commuted to the office by bike for about 18 months before I purchased another car. During one of my rides into the office, I came up with an idea to rebrand my law firm with a brand name that I thought might make it more appealing to entrepreneurs throughout Virginia. I changed the name of my firm to the "Virginia Entrepreneur Law Office" and adopted the acronym "VELO" as part of the re-branding (coincidentally, "velo" is the French word for bicycle). I bought the velo.com domain name, designed new letterhead, created a "VELO" logo where the "O" was a computer start button, printed new business cards, changed my email address, and even printed performance t-shirts with the new logo and domain name.

I held onto this branding for several years, but no one ever "got it." Whenever someone was referred to me, my referral sources always used my name and not my firm's new brand name. Many times, my new VELO branding initially resulted in confusion when I would answer the phone with "VELO" or "Virginia Entrepreneur Law Office" and then had to explain that, yes, they had actually reached Joel Ankney's law office. After a few years of this struggle, I finally realized that my name is my brand because (1) prospective clients were referred to me because of my personal reputation, not my corporate branding, and (2) I have a unique name. As a result, I changed the name of my law firm back to "Law Office of Joel Ankney PC" and shortened the branding to "Ankney Law" to help reduce client confusion.

I see other lawyers and law firms now adopting brand names rather than using the names of the lawyers who own them. Perhaps that branding tactic works for them, but in my experience, most clients engage the lawyer for who they are, not because of the brand name. For all but the biggest law firms, brand recognition is attached to the lawyer's name, not a corporate brand.

Spin-off Special Branding

A few years after changing the name of my firm back to my name, I came up with another marketing idea: what if I virtually spun off my entity formation services and advertised and marketed them under a different brand? The Law Office of Joel Ankney PC would continue to exist and have its own website, letterhead, and other marketing materials, but I would create a new website with a unique brand to advertise entity formation services to potential clients throughout Virginia. And so, "Virginia Startups" was created.

I bought the virginiastartups.com domain name; created a new website for business entity formation services, a flat fee pricing schedule, and new letterhead; ordered new business cards; and, yes, ordered some cool "Get Started with Virginia Startups" t-shirts. It was like launching a new business with no brand recognition. It never took off. People still referred to me by my name, even for business entity formation services. Even when I provided formation services using the Virginia Startups letterhead, email address, and branded legal documents, everyone still recognized that they were engaging "Joel Ankney," not a business owned by Joel that was branded as "Virginia Startups."

Perhaps I could have pushed the branding effort more by buying online advertising, attending or sponsoring local startup events under the "Virginia Startups" brand name, or through some other brand-building efforts, but it just seemed more effective to continue to market under my personal name. So, I abandoned "Virginia Startups" after about 18 months. I retained the virginiastartups.com domain name for several more years and had it redirect to my law firm's website, but eventually abandoned it because no one was entering my website through that domain name.

This was the second time I learned that I am my own brand and that trying to rebrand without using my name was too confusing to existing and prospective clients. As a result of these experiments, I'm sticking with my name for my law firm.

Free Seminars

When I started my solo practice, I discovered a consultant who was a proponent of education-based marketing for lawyers. I joined his email list and enjoyed his emails for many years because they contained many ideas about how a lawyer could market their practice by educating people about the law they practiced. As I recall, he suggested providing free seminars on legal topics to the local community. For example, a lawyer might offer a free seminar on Wills at a 55 and over community. The theory was that providing free seminars would draw in people who would naturally want to engage you for legal services after they learned about the topic, realized they needed a lawyer to help them, and saw you demonstrate your expertise.

This sounded like a good idea, so I offered a free seminar on how to start a corporation or limited liability company. I rented a large meeting room at the main library in my city and advertised my free seminar on the local newspaper's online events calendar. On the day of the seminar, I picked up some trays of cookies and paper products to provide refreshments. Only six people showed up, and none were looking to engage a lawyer. Instead, they were looking for free legal advice on how to start their businesses. The seminar quickly devolved into a question-and-answer session, with each person asking specific questions about their business and looking for detailed advice. I was new to marketing outside of the big law firm, so I probably failed to keep control of the seminar, and that's on me. However, I also discovered that offering free seminars is only valuable if you can attract a group of your ideal prospective clients. If not, you're simply giving out free legal advice to people who don't want to engage a lawyer.

Free Consultations

Lawyers with certain types of practices, such as personal injury and personal bankruptcy, have normalized the practice of offering free consultations to prospective clients. You will have to decide whether you will be one of those lawyers. I have learned that I am not. When I began my solo practice, I offered free consultations because I thought that would be an excellent way to attract new clients. What I soon discovered is that prospective clients would come for the free consultation and then never come back. They also never referred anyone else to me. The return on that marketing tactic was basically zero, so I abandoned it.

Instead, I have followed the example of some of my colleagues and offered an initial consultation at half my hourly rate so that the prospective client has some investment in the meeting. We will move forward at my full hourly rate if they engage me. If they don't engage me, I've made a fee for my time, so it's not a complete loss, and I feel freer with my advice during the consultation because I know I'm getting paid something for it.

The type of law you practice might dictate whether you should provide free consultations. Experiment with them and decide for yourself. However, in my experience, free consultations do not bring value to my type of law practice.

Selling My Resume

Resumes help get you a job, not clients. The big law firms I worked for encouraged detailed information on each lawyer's biographical page on its website. Just browse the lawyer profiles of any big law firm's website, and you'll see what I mean. You will see education, academic achievements, awards, speaking engagements, representative cases, and so on. As a result, when I left Troutman Sanders to start my solo practice, I felt prospective clients would look closely at my resume when deciding whether to engage me.

While I'm uncomfortable waving my resume around for everyone to see, I believe it contains some impressive achievements that I thought would attract clients. I graduated first in my class from a well-respected law school, am a member of the Order of the Coif, was on the Law Review, and had my student Note published in my school's Law Review. I've worked at two large national law firms and handled significant projects there, even as a young associate. I was an adjunct professor at William & Mary Law School for five years, teaching entertainment transactions. I've published two books, one of which has gained national attention in the Entrepreneurship Through Acquisition community. Virginia lawyers have selected me as a Virginia Legal Elite lawyer for intellectual property law and business law multiple times.

I used to put all this information on my website's About page, but I've discovered that prospective clients looking for a business lawyer don't understand what any of it means. None of it helps a prospective client understand what I can do for them. You can still find some of this information on my website, but I have tried to pare it down, make it more understandable, and include only information that I think will help a prospective client decide to engage me. I found that my resume may not be as important to a prospective client as it is to my colleagues in the legal community, so I don't put much emphasis on publishing a detailed one. Of course, you will need to determine whether prospective clients looking to engage a lawyer for your services might look for your resume before you decide to abandon that marketing tactic like I did.

Recognition Awards

I have earned awards during my career. For example, multiple times, I have been named a "Virginia Elite" lawyer by Virginia Business Magazine and a "Top Lawyer of Coastal Virginia" by Coastal Virginia Magazine. Like much of the information I used to include on my resume, however, I have found that prospective clients looking for a business lawyer don't understand those recognition awards and don't select a business lawyer based on them. As a result, just like with my resume, I don't put much emphasis on recognition awards (I'll still accept them, but I don't publicize them much). Once again, you will need to determine whether prospective clients looking to engage a lawyer for your services might look to see if you have received any recognition awards before you decide to abandon that marketing tactic as I did.

Bar and Government Leadership

When I was a lawyer at Hunton & Williams and Mays & Valentine, I was appointed to serve on two legislative committees for the Virginia General Assembly. Richmond, Virginia, was in the process of developing a biotechnology office park. Hunton & Williams was heavily involved in state politics and regulation and wanted some of its lawyers to serve on a legislative committee considering and drafting first-of-its-kind legislation to regulate biotechnology research and testing in Virginia. The hope was that new biotechnology companies would relocate to Richmond because of industry-friendly legislation. I worked for months on this committee, even helping to draft the proposed legislation and participating on a panel for a question-and-answer session about the legislation. The General Assembly enacted the legislation, and I was at the governor's signing ceremony (I even got my picture taken with the governor). I've never had a client engage me in my private practice because of my participation on this committee.

A few years after that, I was invited to sit on a legislative committee tasked with making recommendations to the General Assembly about whether to consider regulating internet use in Virginia. My invitation came because of the development of my intellectual property practice at Mays & Valentine and the firm's connections to the General Assembly. I participated in several public hearings where the committee took public comments about regulating internet usage. The committee then drafted a report to the General Assembly reporting those comments, the committee's findings, and the committee's recommendations. Based on our report, I recall that the General Assembly decided to take no action. I've never had a client engage me because of my work on that committee.

One of the first things I did when I started my solo practice was to join my local bar association. I wanted to use the local bar association to connect with other small firm lawyers and create referral relationships. I felt I could improve my chances of meeting and working with other lawyers by joining a bar association committee. The bar association had about ten committees. I felt my experience would fit best on the bar's Technology Committee.

I phoned the bar's executive committee liaison for the Technology Committee and asked him if I could join. He called me back later and asked if I would chair the Technology Committee, which I reluctantly accepted. The bar association gave my committee a budget, and I spent the next year working with a website developer to develop a new and improved website for the bar association where, among other things, members could search a membership directory and renew their membership online. I've never had a lawyer refer a client to me or had a client engage me because of this experience.

I don't regret these experiences, but I recognize that if they were marketing tactics, they weren't very effective.

I am not discouraging bar or government leadership, but in my practice, I haven't seen that type of volunteer service result in new clients or more legal work. So, if you want to join and participate in a bar or government leadership, you probably should do so for reasons other than marketing your law practice.

Networking Organizations

I have frequently been invited to attend and join business networking associations, such as Business Network International (BNI), when a businessperson learns I am a business lawyer. I've joined and participated in a few, especially when I was starting my solo practice. I quickly discovered that the other networking group members and prospective clients they could refer to me didn't coincide with my target client audience. In addition, many people in these groups wanted me to refer them to all my clients even though I didn't know them well and had no experience with their work. I wasn't making the kind of connections I had hoped for, so I abandoned those groups to use my time to discover and implement more effective marketing tactics.

Social Media

I have personal social media accounts to share my life with family and friends who don't live near me. I have experimented with the idea of having separate social media accounts for my law practice. I have abandoned that idea for two reasons.

First, it takes too much of my time (i.e., non-billable time) to regularly create content for, update, and maintain practice-related social media accounts. An account that is not regularly updated seems stale and might be a turnoff to prospective clients.

Second, and more importantly, my target audience for potential clients typically does not search for or select a lawyer for a small business or real estate transaction using social media. Likewise, my target clients are unlikely to contact or engage a business lawyer as a result of an advertisement on social media.

I'm not against marketing or advertising on social media. It appears effective for lawyers with certain types of practices, such as personal injury, criminal defense, traffic, and divorce and custody. So, again, I'm not telling you not to use social media for finding legal work, but prior to launching that effort, seriously consider the social media platforms on which your existing and prospective clients might be spending their time and focus your efforts on those platforms. I have observed that many lawyers feel the need to be on as many social media platforms as possible, which can multiply your content creation and posting burdens without regard for whether your target audience of prospective clients select lawyers from content or ads posted on each of those platforms.

Contrary to conventional wisdom (i.e., the "wisdom" of those selling their services as digital marketers), I believe you can make a decision quickly about whether social media advertising is working for you based on short-term costs and results, including fees for advertising, the time you must spend to create content regularly, the quantity of inquiries for your services, and the type of client and work for which they might engage you.

Online Advertising

I'm online, I just don't advertise online. I have a website that contains a blog, and I have a YouTube channel with informational videos, but I don't pay for online advertising, such as Google Ads. I experimented with digital advertising, but quickly concluded it was not for me for three reasons. First, my target audience of potential clients overlaps with the same types of clients big law firms are seeking. Buying attention online is expensive. I discovered that it is too expensive for my solo practice to bid against big law firms for online ads to reach that audience. Second, my research indicates that gaining online recognition through digital advertising takes a long time, which would increase the spend on advertisements. Third, I discovered that the people who did contact me as the result of a digital advertisement were not serious potential clients, but simply looking for free legal advice. There was no ROI for me from digital advertising.

These marketing tactics didn't work for me, but that's not to say they won't work for you. Don't be afraid to experiment with different marketing tactics to determine what works for you.

I'm not afraid to try out new marketing tactics, but my practice has limited time and cash resources, so I need to constantly evaluate whether the effort and expense is worth the return. Making decisions quickly about whether to continue or abandon a marketing tactic seems counterintuitive to my observation in Chapter 4 about giving marketing tactics time to mature, grow, and bear fruit. In my experience, however, regular, frequent evaluations of marketing tactics provide enough evidence to help me decide whether to continue or abandon a particular marketing tactic.

My biggest metrics in determining whether to continue or abandon a marketing tactic are, in no particular order:

- Where are current and potential clients looking for information about lawyers or legal services?

- How much is the tactic costing me in money?

- How much is the tactic costing me in time?

- What type of people are initially responding to the tactic?

- What type of projects are people engaging me for because of the tactic?

- How many desirable potential clients are responding to the tactic?

- What amount of legal fees am I collecting from the clients who engage me because of the tactic?

- Is the content I'm providing vulnerable due to the platform's decisions? Do I own and control the content produced, or does the platform control the content in a manner that might decrease its visibility to prospective clients for reasons outside my control?

All our resources are limited. I have a limited marketing budget and limited time to work on non-billable marketing tactics because I need to focus on billable work to bring in revenue.

I prefer to attract clients who have the resources to afford my fees, I prefer to attract projects that earn a larger aggregate fee, and I prefer to be paid when I invoice my client for my fees (chasing non-paying clients is annoying and takes me away from the clients and projects I enjoy).

I am not afraid to abandon a marketing tactic, even if I have already invested money and time into it. That money and time are sunk costs. There is much debate about whether the concept of sunk costs is valid, but I'm not an economist and this book is not the forum for that debate. The concept, whether valid or not, helps me psychologically move on quickly when I decide to abandon a marketing tactic, so it works well for me.

Long before becoming a lawyer, I learned to let go of money and time invested into any effort that didn't produce the desired results. I don't consider the money or time wasted because I usually learn something from an abandoned marketing tactic, which helps me iterate to the next one. So, if you think about it from that perspective, no money or time is ever actually lost.

FIFTEEN

Before You Start Looking for Rain

MARKETING ADVICE TO MY YOUNGER SELF

I started practicing law in my late twenties. I am several decades older now as I write this book. Over the past 30 years, I've learned a lot about getting clients and legal work.

If my current self could talk with my twenty-something self about getting clients for my private law practice, I would share the following thoughts to give my younger self a head start at becoming a rain catcher:

- There isn't one correct way to market your legal practice. Marketing tactics can be as unique as each lawyer.

- You don't have to be an extrovert or act like an extrovert to get clients or legal work.

- You can use your strengths, such as writing, teaching, producing quality legal work, learning, and creating one-on-one relationships through these efforts, to get clients and legal work.

- The only thing time does is pass. Spend a lot of your time generating marketing ideas. Going through this exercise will spark new ideas in you more than implementing them will, but the sooner you get out of ideation and planning mode and start trying marketing tactics, the sooner you will either get new clients and work or be able to determine whether to iterate on or abandon a marketing tactic and move on to another one.

- Something is better than nothing. This concept goes hand in hand with the preceding concept. Always be engaged in some marketing tactic. Often, even unsuccessful marketing tactics will be steppingstones to successful ones as you refine your marketing ideas and tactics based on the experience you gain.

- You don't need to spend much money to obtain clients, but you do need to invest considerable time.

- When you are a young lawyer at a big law firm, focus on marketing yourself internally to other lawyers and established firm clients.

- It's all about respectful relationships.

- Be genuine.

- Pursue marketing tactics that align with your personality and style. For me, writing and publishing to educate people about legal issues has become one of the best ways to market my legal services in alignment with my personality.

- Put 80% of your effort into the 20% of marketing tactics that work.

- Study marketing. Borrow marketing ideas from non-legal businesses. How do other businesses market their services or products? Evaluate whether you might borrow some of those tactics for yourself.

- Continuously try out new ideas and evaluate current marketing tactics.

- Determine what metrics you will use to evaluate the success of your marketing tactics. Will it be billable hours? Legal fees? New clients? New projects from existing clients? The type of legal work you are receiving? The type of clients you are serving? Or any combination of these?

- Evaluate marketing tactics quickly and abandon them if they aren't working.

- If a marketing tactic appears to generate some preliminary results, give it appropriate time to mature.

- Be patient. Marketing is like farming. Most effective marketing tactics don't pay off right away. Most of the time, you will plant seeds and water them. You will harvest the legal work when your seeds ripen into fruit. It might take three months or ten years (or more) for a seed (or relationship) to ripen and be harvested.

- Don't do just one thing. Diversify your marketing tactics. Some may bear fruit sooner than others. Having marketing tactics that mature into legal projects at different time frames should provide a steady stream of legal work.

- When you get a new client or project, look backward and map how that client or project came to you. Understanding that process will help you determine which marketing tactics are working. It's difficult to create a map to an objective you haven't seen yet, but easy to look backward to see how you arrived there.

- Marketing is an incremental exercise. Consistent "small" efforts can turn into big results.

- Learn how to develop a marketing plan early in your career, then make one, implement it, measure its effectiveness, and adapt it as your career progresses. The data you collect on the efficacy of your marketing tactics will drive updates and revisions to your marketing plan.

- Get help. As brilliant as you think you are, you would be foolish not to try to learn and build on the experiences and ideas of others. Ask others to help you generate and vet your marketing ideas. You will find that, in many instances, input from others will help you refine your ideas and marketing tactics in ways that will increase your success. Get input from lawyers and non-lawyers (especially those with marketing training or experience). Each will have different perspectives and experiences.

- Attract champions. Champions are people who will talk about you and your work when you are not present.

Above all, give yourself permission to be who you are and to develop marketing tactics that capitalize on your unique strengths. I have gradually allowed myself this permission during my career, which has resulted in a slow adoption of marketing tactics that align with my personality.

I believe that my law practice would have grown faster if I had received this permission while in law school or at the beginning of my legal career, although that's a difficult prediction to make without the hindsight of how my marketing tactics have brought me new clients and legal work over three decades of my legal career.

Legal marketing is an essential part of private practice. You must learn how to do it to survive, regardless of whether you are a solo practitioner or a lawyer in any size law firm. The sooner you take marketing seriously in your career, the faster you will see your practice grow.

I hope that the experiences and results I share in this book will give you confidence that using your strengths to market your law practice will bring you similar results so that you will feel comfortable developing and implementing your unique marketing tactics as soon as possible.

Also by Joel Ankney

Here's the Deal: Everything You Wish a Lawyer
Would Tell You About Buying a Small Business

Before You Leap: Your Legal Guide
to Starting a Freelancing Business